COCKTAILS

Galore

COCKTAILS

Galore

Kate Moseley

spruce

An Hachette UK Company
www.hachette.co.uk

First published in Great Britain in 2006 by
Spruce,
a division of Octopus Publishing Group Ltd
Endeavour House
189 ShaftesburyAvenue
London
WC2H 8JY
www.octopusbooks.co.uk
www.octopusbooks.usa.com

This edition published in 2013

ISBN 978-1-84601-446-8

A CIP catalogue record for this book is available
from the British Library

Printed and bound in China

CONTENTS

Introduction 6

Vodka 22

Gin 46

Rum 68

Tequila 88

Whiskey 102

Brandy 118

Best of the Rest 140

Nonalcoholic 164

Index 188

EQUIPMENT

Learn about the essential equipment needed to mix the perfect cocktail, and you will soon become the experienced bartender that you aspire to be!

★ CORKSCREW ★

You won't be opening any bottles of wine without it!

★ PITCHER ★

This is invaluable for making large quantities of punch or cocktails to serve to groups.

★ COCKTAIL SHAKER ★

There are several types of cocktail shaker to choose from, but the two most common are the standard and the Boston. The standard usually comes in chrome but can be made from toughened plastic. The base, also known as the "can," resembles a tall, cone-shaped tumbler. It has a tight fitting funnel top with built-in strainer holes on which the cap fits snugly. The Boston shaker comprises a tall metal beaker and a plain glass

beaker which fits tightly inside it. The metal beaker has a pouring hole, often with a built-in strainer and cap. The glass beaker can also be used as a mixing glass. Both are efficient and easy to keep clean.

★ COCKTAIL STRAINER ★

The Boston shaker is used in conjunction with a cocktail- or "Hawthorne" strainer. This comes in two parts: a frame, and an edge of wire coil to prevent spillage. The protruding prongs balance on the rim of the cocktail shaker. The strainer (inserted inside the shaker) is held firmly and the liquid is poured out between the prongs. Perforations allow the liquid to pass through without the ice falling into the glass. For even finer straining, use a fine mesh sieve or a tea strainer held just above the glass.

★ CITRUS ZESTER ★

A small tool usually having a line of five small rings on the top set at an angle. These are, in fact, quite sharp and when held firmly against the skin of the citrus fruit and dragged downward, or toward you, will form fine lines of zest.

★ PESTLE AND MORTAR ★

A mortar is a bowl-like vessel made of hard material, usually ceramic or marble, that is used for crushing or grounding ingredients with the pestle—a club-shaped, handheld tool. Avoid using wooden mortars which taint easily when used with wet ingredients and can be unhygienic.

★ CITRUS JUICER ★

Freshly squeezed lemon, orange, and lime are far superior to anything ready prepared in a bottle. Electric spinning juicers are ideal for making big batches, but be careful not to overdo it and grind the pith as well which makes the juice, and so the drink, bitter. A simple stainless steel or glass lemon squeezer is fine for the job. Make sure it has a good lip for catching the juice and enough "teeth" or a good strainer to catch the pips. You'll get more juice from your fruit if you roll the fruit first on your bar chopping board with the palm of your hand, applying gentle pressure. When you cut the fruit in half the juice should be released more easily. Heating whole or halved fruit for a few seconds in a dish in the microwave will also make them juicier, but watch out as the fruit and juice will be warm. Although juice extraction seems tedious, the flavor in the cocktail makes it all worthwhile. Bottled or canned juices can be too sweet or contain preservatives that taint the flavor. If fresh juice makes the drink too sharp, add a little sugar syrup.

★ STIRRING ROD ★

A glass stick used for stirring drinks with ice in the mixing glass. Especially useful for mixing carbonated cocktails and martinis.

★ BAR SPOON ★

The classic bar spoon has a long handle (about 10 inches/25cm), with an oval or teardrop shaped bowl. It can be used as a spoon measure (slightly larger than the average teaspoon) as well as for stirring drinks and muddling ingredients. The best ones have a twisted stem (or barley/spiral effect) and a flat end to prevent them from slipping. They are easier to grip than their smooth-stemmed counterparts.

★ MUDDLER ★

This is a short, rounded, wooden "baton," similar to a pestle but with a flat end. It is used to mash sugar and Angostura bitters, or sugar and fresh mint, until the sugar dissolves. It may also be used for crushing fruit in a glass by pushing down on it with a twisting action, or for crushing ice cubes. Alternatively, use a pestle and mortar, the end of a small rolling pin in a bowl, or the heel of a mixing spoon.

★ ICE CREAM SCOOP ★

If you fancy serving ice cream or sorbet cocktails, a metal scoop is the best to use because it's quick and

easy to clean. Just dip it in hot water before scooping the ice cream into the drink. Always put the ice cream straight back into the freezer after taking the scoops.

★ MIXING GLASS ★

A straight, plain, glass pitcher with a lip for pouring, used to chill a cocktail as quickly as possible. It should be large enough to take 1½ pints (24fl oz/750ml) of fluid. Don't be tempted to buy a colored or patterned glass pitcher—a clear mixing glass will allow you to see if any "foreign bodies" have fallen into the cocktail by mistake. Alternatives include a straight water pitcher, a clear glass bottle, a measuring pitcher, or the glass beaker from a Boston shaker.

★ JIGGER AND PONY ★

The standard measure for ingredients is known as a "jigger" and holds 1½fl oz/45ml. Another standard measure is a "pony" which measures 2 tablespoons or 1fl oz/30ml. Measures are available in other sizes and are often called "shots." A shot, ideally, is 1fl oz/30ml. If you don't have a measure, a standard liqueur glass will be fine to use. In fact, anything can be used as a measure as long as it is used consistently throughout the recipe to keep the proportions right. A clean medicine measure, the cap off a bottle, or half an egg cup are other suggestions.

★ MEASURING SPOONS ★

Measuring spoons come in sets of ⅙fl oz, ⅓fl oz and ½fl oz (5ml, 10ml and 15ml) in stainless steel or plastic.

★ CHOPPING BOARD AND FRUIT KNIFE ★

A small wooden board and sharp stainless knife are required for cutting and preparing fruit for garnishing.

★ BLENDER/LIQUIDIZER ★

Only use a domestic food blender if it is equipped to cope with crushing ice. If not, consider investing in a commercial blender. It is still preferable to use cracked or crushed ice as this will save wear and tear on the blender's blades and motor. A good blender should have several speeds or action settings, a goblet made of heavy-duty glass, plastic, or stainless steel, and detachable blades to enable thorough cleaning. (Use a bottlebrush for safety and speed when cleaning the blades.) When using the blender to make cocktails, measure in the ingredients, then add crushed ice and start the machine on slow speed, building up speed to produce a smooth, even consistency. Strain into a glass and serve immediately.

★ ICE BUCKET ★

The better the ice bucket is insulated, the longer the ice will last. Keep the lid on and use a good pair of tongs to lift the ice out.

★ PARING KNIFE ★

A small sharp knife used for taking a thin layer of citrus peel in strands, or parings, from the fruit. Also useful for cutting wedges and other fruit shapes.

★ CANELLE KNIFE ★

A small tool with a grooved attachment on top used to cut citrus spirals. Hold this against the fruit and steadily drag it round the fruit to get a spiral of peel, thicker and more robust than when using a zester.

★ COCKTAIL STICKS ★

Small wooden or plastic sticks of varying colors, plain or with decorative ends, are used to spear maraschino cherries, olives, small onions, or slices of fruit for garnishing cocktails. Plastic sticks can be reused after sterilization, whereas the wooden variety should be thrown away.

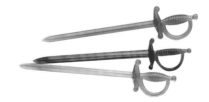

GLASSES

Serving cocktails is as much about presentation and pizzazz as it is about content. So make sure you know your Boston from your Collins.

★ BRANDY SNIFTER ★

Short stemmed with a large balloon-like bowl. Traditionally used for brandy and some liqueurs. The bulbous cup is designed to let the hand warm the drink while the cup shape wafts the tantalizing aroma to your nose.

★ OLD-FASHIONED GLASS ★

Also known as tumbler, lowball, whiskey or rocks glass. Short, broad, flat-bottomed glass, essential for serving any drink "on the rocks" (with ice).

★ CHAMPAGNE FLUTE ★

This tall, elegant glass is an excellent way to serve champagne, as it both showcases the wine's bouquet while retaining the bubbles for longer due to its small surface area.

★ HIGHBALL GLASS ★

A clear, simple, tall glass used for any drink containing alcohol and a mixer and served with ice, such as gin and tonic or a Harvey Wallbanger.

★ COLLINS GLASS ★

Taller and thinner than the highball, the Collins glass is often frosted or pebbled with a smooth rim. Perfect for serving a Tom Collins, this glass is also used for fizzes and tropical drinks.

★ MARGARITA GLASS OR COUPETTE ★

Larger and rounder than the traditional cocktail glass, the Margarita has a unique double bowl. Used for Margaritas and Daiquiris.

★ BOSTON GLASS ★

Tall, slightly conical highball glass.

★ CHAMPAGNE SAUCER ★

Commonly used for serving champagne, but this elegant glass allows the bubbles and bouquet of the drink to escape faster than the champagne flute.

★ COCKTAIL GLASS ★

Classic, stemmed glass, often referred to as a "Martini" glass. Used for serving drinks "straight up" (without ice), the slender stem of the cocktail glass prevents the heat of your hand from warming the contents as you sip. Always chill before using.

★ GOBLET ★

Short, bowl-shaped glass with foot and short stem.

★ TODDY GLASS ★

Short heatproof glass used to serve toddies made of liquor, hot water, and spices.

★ SHOT GLASS ★

A tiny glass, often called a "jigger" used for measuring and serving short drinks with a high alcohol content called "shooters."

★ WINEGLASS ★

The white wineglass is slightly smaller than the red wineglass, which has a rounder, more balloon-like shape.

★ SLING ★

A tall and often stemmed glass similar to a Collins glass, also known as a Catalina glass.

★ IRISH COFFEE GLASS ★

Thick, heatproof glass with foot, short stem, and glass handle used for serving hot coffee mixed with a liqueur.

TRICKS OF THE TRADE

There are some clever tricks that every expert mixologist should know. Here are some useful tips.

★ SUGAR SYRUP ★

Some cocktails taste better with a little added sweetness to counteract the "sour" of fresh fruit juice. Try sprinkling a sugar cube with Angostura bitters, placing it in a glass and stirring. Alternatively, bruise sugar and fresh fruit or mint leaves with a muddler to make a paste, which can be added to the cocktail. You may like to buy "simple syrup" or "sirop de gomme," which come in a variety of flavors including almond (orgeat), coconut, cassis, framboise, grenadine, and vanilla. Make your own sugar syrup by measuring two parts superfine sugar to one part water into a pan. Stir over a gentle heat then bring to a boil for 3–5 minutes. The longer you boil it, the more concentrated it will become. Cool, then pour into a bottle and refrigerate. It is best used within 4 days. For variation, flavor the syrup with spices (for example cinnamon sticks, star anise, or fresh root ginger), lemongrass, or lime leaves.

★ CREAM COCKTAILS ★

Rich and creamy, these cocktails were traditionally served at the end of a meal. These days, if you feel like one, any time is fine! Cream will mix with most liqueurs and can mask the harshness of alcohol, leaving a drink smooth enough to slide easily down the throat. Always use heavy cream to give the cocktail enough body. Be aware that the action of acid from fruit juices can react with the cream and make it look, and possibly taste, curdled if it is left to stand. For this reason it is important to serve the cocktail as soon as it has been made. Always keep the cream refrigerated and wash the bar equipment thoroughly after making cream cocktails.

★ LAYERING (POUSSE-CAFÉ) ★

The pousse-café is a multi-colored layered drink, served in a shot glass. Its success depends on the knowledge and skill of the bartender. Each ingredient is carefully poured into the glass, either down a bar spoon, with the flat end in contact with the surface of the previous ingredient, letting it flow slowly over the top, or over a spoon in contact with the side of the glass and the surface of the drink. Ingredients must be layered according to their alcoholic density. Generally, the higher the density, the lighter the liquid and the more likely it is to float. Start with the non-alcoholic ingredients—such as syrups, which are heavy and will stay at the bottom—then work up to the strongest, lightest liquids. The exception is cream and cream liqueurs, which will rise naturally to the top (like the cream on the top of unhomogenized milk). Like any skill, layering takes practice...but therein lies the fun!

★ FLAMING DRINKS ★

Care must be taken when igniting drinks. Make sure that there is plenty of space around the glass and that you don't knock it over accidentally. Never carry a drink that is alight. Extinguish the flames by covering the glass gently with a metal tray. Warn the drinker that the rim will be hot, and let it sit a while so that lips are not burned! In order to light a drink, the top layer should be a spirit containing at least 40% alcohol.

★ SHAKING ★

Shaking a drink with crushed or cubed ice will both chill and dilute it. The more ice you use, the less the drink will be diluted. (Using too little ice will dilute a drink faster than using more since the smaller quantity melts more rapidly.) For best results, fill the cocktail shaker two-thirds full with fresh ice, then add the fruit juices, eggs, or cream, and finally the liquor. Attach the top and cap firmly and, holding the shaker in front of you with one hand firmly clasping the top and the other hand supporting the base, shake the cocktail using a brisk pumping action. Practice this before doing it in front of people in case your hands slip and the cocktail shaker falls apart all over your guests! After shaking for about fifteen seconds, remove the cap and keep holding the top on while you pour the cocktail through the strainer into the glass. Never shake fizzy ingredients.

★ STIR IT UP ★

Stirring is best done in a lipped mixing glass, in the glass half of a Boston shaker, or in a pitcher with a capacity of at least 1 pint (16fl oz/500ml). Place cracked or cubed ice in the glass, add the ingredients, then stir the drink with a bar spoon, sliding the back of the spoon down the inside of the mixing glass and twirling it gently between thumb and forefinger. When stirring drinks with soda or other fizzy liquids the drink will hold its effervescence longer if stirred gently for just a brief time—but don't be too energetic in the stirring! When the glass starts to show condensation on the outside, the drink is chilled and ready for pouring. Use a Hawthorne strainer when pouring the drink into a glass. Only drinks with clear ingredients should be stirred, the rest should be shaken.

★ FROSTING RIMS ★

For added effect, decorate the top of the glass with salt, sugar, chocolate, or even desiccated coconut. The salt frosting on the rim of a margarita glass is achieved by taking a wedge of lime or lemon and running it around the rim of the glass while holding the glass upside down to prevent juice going into the glass or down the stem. Next, dip the glass rim gently into a saucer of salt until evenly coated. For sugary frostings, dip the rim of the glass into the whipped white of an egg or a wet sponge, then into a saucer of sugar. Repeat the procedure a couple of times for an even coating. For an even greater effect, match the sugar color to the flavor or color of the drink by mixing it with a few drops of vegetable dye or a colored syrup—such as grenadine. Sugar frosting should only be used for sweetened cocktails.

★ CHILLING ★

It's vital that a cocktail is served cold. Glasses can be chilled in the fridge, if you have room, or more rapidly in the freezer. If possible, keep the cocktail shaker chilled too. Alternatively, fill the cocktail glass with ice before use. (Cracked or crushed ice is better for quicker, more even chilling.) It may take a few minutes for the condensation to appear on the glass to show that it is chilled, but this gives you time to prepare and mix the remainder of the ingredients. When the glass is suitably frosted, discard the chilling ice, and pour in your cocktail. Some drinks also call for the liquid ingredients to be chilled or frozen. Spirits such as vodka change viscosity if placed in the freezer for a time and so can give a very different texture to a drink.

★ NICE ICE ★

Ice is the essential cocktail ingredient. A committed bartender will make ice with bottled mineral or spring water, which tastes purer, and stays clearer when frozen. If you're planning to make lots of cocktails, buy bags of ice from your local supermarket or liquor store. Don't be mean when you are putting ice in a drink. Two cubes won't do—you must fill the glass to keep the drink really cold. There's safety in numbers—the more ice cubes, the longer they will take to melt and dilute the drink. Once ice has been used in a cocktail shaker or for chilling glasses, discard it and use fresh for the next drink. Ice can be crushed by hitting the bag of ice, wrapped in dish towel, with a rolling pin. Alternatively, use an electric ice crusher, or a blender that can take the strain. Crack using an ice pick.

★ INFUSIONS ★

Any spirit with an alcohol content of 40% or more can be flavored with fruit or spices to give an extra dimension to your cocktails—but it can't be done in a hurry. One exception is chili-flavored vodka. Just add a few slices of fresh chili to the cocktail shaker with the vodka and it will impart the "heat" in a few shakes! Vodka is an ideal base to infuse because it has little flavor of its own. Try it with fruits such as lemon, raspberries, redcurrants, or cranberries. Add sugar to the spirits along with the fruit or lemon parings to make it sweeter and help release the flavors. Macerate for between two and six weeks, depending on the fruit, and shake daily to help dissolve the sugar. Sloes or damsons, in gin, are best left for twelve weeks. Strawberries and cherries are great in brandy, and split vanilla pods added to a bottle of rum add a sweetness that is wonderful in daiquiris. Herbs such as rosemary, bay leaves, or thyme, and spices such as cinnamon, or lemongrass, can also be used to flavor vodka, gin, or whiskey.

★ BUILDING ★

This simply means to mix the drink directly in the serving glass. Fill the chosen glass with ice and add each ingredient straight to the glass. Stir before serving.

★ DOUBLE STRAINING ★

Fruit and flecks of ice are removed from a drink by pouring the cocktail from the shaker through its strainer and then through a tea strainer.

★ DUSTING ★

This is where you are instructed to dust an ingredient such as cocoa powder, ground cinnamon, or ground nutmeg over the surface of the drink.

★ FLOATING ★

To float cream on the surface of a drink, whip the cream so that it still has a liquid quality but is thicker than pouring cream. Stir the drink to create a whirlpool effect and pour the cream over a spoon which is in contact with the drink's surface.

★ FRUIT PURÉES ★

Chop your fruit into small pieces and process (without ice) in a blender on a high speed. You may want to adjust the sweetness using some sugar syrup. You may also need to strain the purée before use to get rid of any pips, seeds, or small lumps of fruit.

★ GLASS HEATING ★

If you are warming a balloon glass in which to serve brandy, you should always place a metal spoon in the glass before adding boiling water. This will help to disperse the heat and prevent the glass from cracking.

★ MUDDLING ★

This is the process by which a fruit or herb is crushed to release its flavors using a blunt-ended instrument, a muddle, which is similar to a pestle.

GARNISHES

Whether it's a simple olive or a montage of fruit kebabs, umbrellas, and multicolored straws, there is no end to the fun you can have with garnishes.

★ CITRUS TWISTS ★

When a recipe calls for a "twist" of orange or lemon, a little of the oil from the rind of the fruit should be added to the cocktail along with the citrus. To make a twist, take a piece of fresh fruit and cut a small oval piece of peel with no pith on it. Holding it over the edge of the glass, twist the peel between the thumb and forefinger. This action releases a fine spray of citrus oil onto the surface of the drink—a truly professional touch! Finally, drop the sliver of fruit into the drink.

★ CITRUS OR VANILLA SPIRAL ★

Use a canelle knife to make citrus peel spirals. Hold the knife against the top of the fruit and steadily drag it round the fruit to get a spiral of peel. Wrap the spiral or even a vanilla bean around a pencil and secure it with a pin, then freeze it for five minutes and the spiral will keep its shape longer in the drink, or when hanging over the side of the glass—as in a "Horse's Neck" cocktail garnish.

★ CUTTING FRUIT WHEELS, WEDGES, AND SLICES ★

Fruit is ideal for decorating cocktails. You can spear it on a cocktail stick and balance it on the top of the glass, or arrange it carefully on the rim. Citrus fruits are the easiest to use, though there are many alternatives. A citrus "wheel" is a whole slice of lemon, lime, or orange. Slices can be twisted or "butterflied" to sit on the glass rim. Alternatively, cut citrus fruits into wedges by topping and tailing the fruit, cutting it in half lengthwise, then cutting each half into four chunky wedges.

★ IMAGINATIVE GARNISHES ★

Some cocktail "pros" shun the use of paper parasols and plastic trinkets for garnishing cocktails, insisting that garnishes should be edible. However, cocktails should be fun, so it's up to you to let your imagination run riot if you want to! Keep garnishing simple with a single pearl onion on a stick for a Gibson, a single green olive for a Dry Martini, a maraschino cherry (available in red, green, yellow, or blue, with or without stalk) a single grape or a trio, or a stem of redcurrants. Lemons, limes, and oranges are standard, but for an elaborate cocktail, use wedges of pineapple or pieces of banana or banana leaf. A natural stirrer can be easily fashioned from a bamboo sprig, a stem of lemongrass, a celery stick, or a length of cucumber. Slivers of chili and slices of cucumber give a savory tang to a drink. Fresh borage, lemon balm, or mint will make refreshing and fragrant additions to a Pimms or a Julep. Fresh rose petals or other edible flowers are perfect delicate garnishes. Mango, watermelon, peach, starfruit, kiwi, apple, raspberries, and strawberries look great if really fresh but, like banana, go brown and become tired looking quite quickly. Decorate with fun swizzle sticks in glass or plastic, straws—small or long, straight, bendy or twisted, plain or stripey—paper parasols or plastic animals and place on smart coasters to really set off the cocktail.

★ CARAMELIZED FRUIT WEDGES ★

To caramelize a wedge of fruit for use as a sweet garnish, sprinkle the surface of the fruit with fine, powdered sugar and glaze it briefly with a hand-held domestic blow torch until the sugar has melted and slightly browned.

★ CINNAMON AND SPICES ★

Cinnamon sticks are ideal for use in hot toddies. Peeled or grated chocolate, ground cinnamon, freshly grated nutmeg, or coffee beans are perfect for sprinkling on creamy cocktails. Sprinkle ground cinnamon through a flame to achieve a crackling, sparkly effect which will impart a wonderful flavor to your drink and looks great too!

★ DECORATED ICE CUBES ★

Fill ice cube trays with water and add a leaf or flower—try lemon balm, basil, mint, lemon verbena, sweet geranium leaves, borage flowers, violas, or pansies. Alternatively, add raspberries, cranberries, redcurrants, black currants, or small segments of lemon, lime, or orange. Star anise or pomegranate seeds look very striking, as do slivers of chili or edible gold leaf.

★ CHILI CURL ★

Slice the bottom end of the chili with a sharp knife five or six times, to leave it in little strands at the end of the chilli. Then, submerge this in water for 2 hours—this will cause the strands to curl outwards leaving you with a fantastic looking chili curl to spice up any cocktail!

★ FLAMED ORANGE TWIST ★

Prepare the "twist" in the same way as above for the citrus twist, but leaving a little pith on the inside of the disc. When you pinch the disc to release the oils do this over the drink and also over a flame. The oil will ignite to give you an impressive flare with a fantastic aroma.

VODKA

AB FAB

INGREDIENTS
1 part Stolichnaya vodka
2 parts cranberry and raspberry juice
Bollinger champagne

Shake the vodka and cranberry juice in a cocktail shaker with cracked ice and strain into a martini glass. Top with champagne. Serve straight up.

TRIVIA
Named after the British TV comedy of the same name, this glamorous combination of Stoli and Bolli was a favorite of the show's character, Patsy.

CAPE CODDER

INGREDIENTS
2 parts vodka
4 parts cranberry juice
2 lime wedges

Pour the vodka and cranberry juice into a highball glass over ice. Squeeze the lime wedges into the drink and drop in. Stir, and serve with straws.

BLOODY MARY

INGREDIENTS

1 part vodka

2 parts tomato juice

¼ part freshly squeezed lemon juice

1 teaspoon Worcestershire sauce

2 dashes of Tabasco sauce

1 pinch celery salt

Shake ingredients gently in a cocktail shaker with cracked ice to keep the tomato juice from separating. Pour into a chilled highball or Collins glass. Garnish with a celery stalk.

TRIVIA

The origins of this famous cocktail remain uncertain. It was allegedly created in 1920 by Ferdinand Petiot at Harry's Bar in Paris. The recipe originally called for vodka and tomato juice in equal parts. Years later, he added Worcestershire sauce, Tabasco sauce, and lemon juice to spice up the drink for New Yorkers when he moved back to the States and worked at the King Cole Bar, St. Regis. Here it was renamed Red Snapper although the name didn't stick. Says Petiot, "One of the boys suggested we call the drink 'Bloody Mary' because it reminded him of the Bucket of Blood Club in Chicago, and a girl there named Mary."

DANGEROUS DETOX

INGREDIENTS

½ part peach schnapps
½ part cranberry juice
½ part vodka
Dash of absinthe

Carefully pour the ingredients into a shot glass in order of density, as listed in the recipe above, so that you have three equal layers and a thin green line of absinthe at the top.

VICTORY COLLINS

INGREDIENTS

1½ parts Stolichnaya Vanil
   (vanilla-flavored vodka)
½ part freshly squeezed lemon juice
1 bar spoon fine white sugar
2 parts grape juice
Orange slices, to garnish

Fill a large highball glass with crushed ice. Shake the vodka, lemon juice, and sugar together (to dissolve) without ice. Pour this mixture over the crushed ice, add the grape juice, and stir. Garnish with slices of orange and serve with straws.

'57 CHEVY

INGREDIENTS

1 part vodka

1 part Southern Comfort

½ part Grand Marnier

2 parts pineapple juice

1 dash freshly squeezed lemon juice

Pineapple wedges, to garnish

Shake all of the ingredients with ice and strain into a highball glass over ice. Garnish with pineapple wedges.

HARVEY WALLBANGER

INGREDIENTS

4 parts orange juice

2 parts vodka

½ part Galliano

Pour the orange juice and the vodka into a highball glass filled with ice. Stir, and then float the Galliano on the top. Garnish with orange slices.

TRIVIA

Renowned bartender Donato "Duke" Antone invented many cocktails in Los Angeles during the 1950s, such as the Rusty Nail, The Godfather, the Flaming Caesar, and the popular Harvey Wallbanger. It is said that a Californian surfer named Harvey lost an important competition and sought consolation in Duke's Blackwatch bar. After one too many Galliano-laced Screwdrivers, Harvey left the bar drunkenly bumping and banging into the walls. He became known as Harvey "The Wallbanger" and thus the eponymous drink was born.

RISING SUN

INGREDIENTS

2 parts vodka
2 parts freshly squeezed grapefruit
   juice
½ part passion fruit syrup
½ lemon, juice only
Pink grapefruit slice, to garnish

Shake all of the ingredients together and strain over ice in a large

old-fashioned glass. Garnish with a slice of pink grapefruit.

AVALON

INGREDIENTS

1½ parts vodka
½ part Pisang Ambon (Dutch
   banana-based liqueur)
2 parts freshly pressed apple juice
1 dash of freshly squeezed lemon juice
Lemonade, to top
Red apple slices, to garnish

Fill a highball glass with ice. Build the vodka, Pisang Ambon, and apple and lemon juice in the glass. Stir and top
with lemonade. Garnish with slices of red apple.

RAPASKA

INGREDIENTS

2 parts Stolichnaya Razberi
   (raspberry-flavored vodka)
1 part passion fruit purée
1 part raspberry purée
½ passion fruit
1 part freshly pressed apple juice
1 part freshly squeezed orange juice
2 raspberries and 1 apple wedge,
   to garnish

Shake all of the ingredients briefly with crushed ice and transfer to a highball glass. Do not strain. Garnish with raspberries and an apple wedge, and serve with straws.

LEMON MERINGUE MARTINI

INGREDIENTS

2 parts citron vodka
1 part Drambuie
1 part freshly squeezed lemon juice
1–2 teaspoons sugar syrup
Lemon twist, to garnish

Shake all ingredients thoroughly with cracked ice in a cocktail shaker. Strain into a cocktail glass. Garnish with a lemon peel twist.

LONG ISLAND ICED TEA

INGREDIENTS

½ part golden rum
½ part gin
½ part vodka
½ part tequila
½ part Cointreau or triple sec
½ part sugar syrup
1 part freshly squeezed lime juice
Cola, to top

Combine all ingredients, except the cola, in a cocktail shaker

with cracked ice. Shake well. Strain into a highball

glass half-filled with ice. Top with a dash of

cola and garnish with a wedge of lime.

TRIVIA

Some claim that this drink was invented during the Prohibition era, as a way of taking the appearance of non-alcoholic iced tea. Others suggest that the Long Island Iced Tea was invented in the late 1970s by Chris Bendicksen, a bartender at the Oak Beach Inn, North (OBI, North) nightclub in Smithtown on Long Island. The drink has a much higher alcohol concentration than most cocktails because of the small amount of mixer.

MUDSLIDE

INGREDIENTS

1 part vodka

1 part Kahlua or coffee liqueur

1 part Irish cream liqueur

Shake ingredients vigorously in a cocktail shaker with cracked ice.

Strain into an old-fashioned glass filled with ice. Garnish with coffee beans.

BUCK'S TWIZZ

INGREDIENTS

1 peeled pink grapefruit slice

1 part Absolut Mandrin
   (orange-flavored vodka)

1 part freshly squeezed orange juice

½ part maraschino liqueur

Champagne, to top

Place the slice of pink grapefruit in the bottom of a large champagne

saucer. Briefly shake the vodka, orange juice, and liqueur with ice and

strain over the grapefruit. Top with champagne, and stir.

TRIVIA

Legend has it that the champagne saucer with its wide, shallow bowl was modeled on the breasts of Marie Antoinette!

IGNORANCE

INGREDIENTS

1 part Ketel One Citroen
  (lemon-flavored vodka)
½ part Campari
½ part passion fruit syrup
2 parts apple juice
1 orange twist, to garnish

Shake all the ingredients with ice and strain over ice into a large old-fashioned glass, or serve straight up,

strained into a chilled martini glass. Garnish with an orange twist.

RED OCTOBER

INGREDIENTS

1 part vodka
2 parts cherry brandy
7-up, to top

Shake the vodka and cherry brandy in a cocktail shaker with cracked ice.

Strain into an old-fashioned glass, half-filled with ice. Top with a little

7-up. Garnish with maraschino cherries.

CHI-CHI

INGREDIENTS

1 1/2 parts vodka

2 parts pineapple juice

1 part coconut cream

1 dash freshly squeezed lime juice

1 pineapple slice and 1 cocktail cherry,
to garnish

Blend the vodka, pineapple juice, coconut cream, and lime juice with a scoop of crushed ice in a blender.

Pour into a coupette or large champagne saucer and garnish with a slice of pineapple and cherry.

CIELO

INGREDIENTS

1 1/2 parts vodka

1 part crème de cassis
(black currant liqueur)

2 dashes of Peychaud's bitters

1/2 lime, juice only

Ginger ale, to top

1 lime wedge, to garnish

TRIVIA

Vodka came from Russia or Poland. Nobody really knows and it's a much debated question. Vodka translates in Russian as "little water" and stems as far back as the 9th century, but vodka as we know it today only appeared in the 18th century when it became possible to purify spirits by filtration.

Build all ingredients over ice in a highball glass, stir, and top with ginger

ale. Garnish with a wedge of lime and serve with straws.

SEA MIST

INGREDIENTS

3 parts cranberry and raspberry juice
3 parts pink grapefruit juice
2 parts vodka
Slices of lime and lemon frozen
    in ice cubes

Shake the fruit juices and vodka thoroughly in a cocktail shaker with

cracked ice. Strain into a highball glass filled with decorated ice cubes.

WHITE RUSSIAN

INGREDIENTS

2 parts vodka
1 part Kahlua or coffee liqueur
1–1½ parts light cream

Shake the vodka and Kahlua in a
cocktail shaker with cracked ice
and strain into an ice-filled
old-fashioned glass. Float the
cream on top using the back
of a bar spoon (see page 15).

TIP
Leave the cream out of a
White Russian and you have
a strong, short, Black Russian.
For a sweeter, more
refreshing option, replace
the cream with cola.

SAKETINI

INGREDIENTS

2 parts sake
1 part vodka
½ part gin
½ part Cointreau or triple sec

Combine the ingredients with cracked ice in a mixing glass.

Stir and strain into a cocktail glass. Serve straight up and garnish

with a slice of cucumber and sliver of scallion.

TRIVIA

Sake is a fermented rice drink from Japan, made much the same way as beer. Rice is malted using a special mold and allowed to ferment before being aged several months. Sake's alcohol content is much higher than beer's, at around 14%. It is one of the oldest known spirits—at least 6,800 years old!

KITSCH REVOLT

INGREDIENTS

1 part Absolut Kurant
   (berry-flavored vodka)
½ part strawberry purée
Champagne, to top
Strawberry slices, to garnish

Shake the vodka and strawberry purée together briefly with ice and strain into a chilled flute. Top with

champagne, stir, and garnish with slices of strawberry.

MOSCOW MULE

INGREDIENTS

1½ parts vodka

1 teaspoon freshly squeezed
   lime juice

Ginger ale, to top

Pour the vodka and the lime juice into a chilled highball glass one-third

filled with ice cubes. Fill the glass to the brim with ginger ale. Garnish

with a slice of lime.

VESPER

INGREDIENTS

1½ parts vodka

1½ parts gin

½ part dry vermouth

1 lemon twist, to garnish

Shake all of the ingredients with ice and double strain

into a chilled martini glass. Garnish with a twist of lemon.

TRIVIA

*This is one drink you have to
serve "James Bond" style—shaken,
not stirred. Bond himself created this
drink in Ian Fleming's Casino Royale of 1953
and named it after the book's femme fatale,
Vesper Lynd. Bond remarked: "I never have
more than one drink before dinner. But I do
like that one to be large, very strong, very
cold, and very well made. I hate small
portions of anything, particularly
when they taste bad."*

BASIL VICE

INGREDIENTS
2 basil leaves
$\frac{1}{2}$ part vodka
Dash of raspberry syrup

Roll the basil leaves up tightly, cut into thin strips and chop finely. Place

them in the bottom of a shot glass, then almost fill with crushed ice. Pour

in the vodka, stir, and add a dash of raspberry syrup.

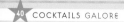

PLASMA

INGREDIENTS

1/2 teaspoon Dijon mustard

1 teaspoon fresh dill, chopped

2 parts Wyborowa Pepper
(pepper-flavored vodka)

2 drops of Tabasco sauce

4 drops of Worcestershire sauce

1/2 lemon, juice only

Celery salt and freshly ground black
pepper, to taste

4 parts tomato juice

Two 6-inch strips of cucumber and
1/2 cherry tomato, to garnish

*"I'll admit it,
I've seen better days.
But I'm still not to be
had for the price of a
cocktail."*
Bette Davis, All
About Eve

Muddle the mustard and dill together in the base of a shaker to form a paste, then add all of the other ingredients with some ice. Shake to mix then strain into a highball glass over ice. Garnish with strips of cucumber and half a seasoned cherry tomato. ● ● ● ➡

POT SHOT

INGREDIENTS

1 lime wedge

1 part Absolut Kurant
(berry-flavored vodka)

1 dash of peach schnapps

Squeeze the lime wedge into a shaker; add the vodka and schnapps, then shake briefly with ice. Strain into a chilled shot glass, and drink it in one gulp.

RUSSIAN SPRING PUNCH

INGREDIENTS

1 part Stolichnaya Vodka

1 part freshly squeezed lemon juice

½ part raspberry purée

½ part crème de cassis
   (black currant liqueur)

1 dash of framboise (raspberry
   liqueur)

1 dash of sugar syrup

Champagne, to top

2 lemon slices and raspberries,
   to garnish

Shake all ingredients except champagne with ice and strain over crushed ice into a sling glass. Top with champagne, stir, and garnish with two lemon slices and fresh raspberries.

GLITTERATI

INGREDIENTS

2 parts vodka

Dash of dry vermouth

A shred of edible gold leaf

Combine the vodka, vermouth, and gold leaf in a mixing glass. Muddle it with some very finely crushed ice to break up the gold leaf. Pour into a cocktail glass and serve straight up. Garnish with a cocktail onion and two black olives. Edible gold leaf is available from good delicatessens and specialist food and drink stores.

DOUBLE VISION

INGREDIENTS

1 part citron vodka
1 part black currant vodka
1 part apple juice
1 part freshly squeezed lime juice
½ part sugar syrup
3 dashes of Angostura bitters
1 apple slice, to garnish

Combine all the ingredients in a cocktail shaker with cracked ice. Shake
well, and strain into a cocktail glass. Serve straight up, garnished with a
thin slice of apple.

MADRAS

INGREDIENTS

2 parts vodka
4 parts cranberry juice
2 parts freshly squeezed orange juice
Orange slices, to garnish

Build all of the ingredients over ice in a highball glass,
stir, and garnish with orange slices. Serve with straws.

TRIVIA

*Cocktails always taste better
when you share them with
someone! The Madras is a perfect
example of a tasty cocktail that serves
a group of people well—simple,
refreshing, and easy to make. Fill a
pitcher with ice, build the
ingredients, stir, and pour.*

POLISH MARTINI

INGREDIENTS

1 part Wyvorowa vodka

1 part Zubrowka Bison grass vodka

Stir both ingredients with ice to chill thoroughly and double strain into

a chilled martini glass. Garnish with a twist of lemon.

COSMOPOLITAN

INGREDIENTS

1½ parts citron vodka

1 part Cointreau or triple sec

1 part cranberry juice

Dash of orange bitters

Dash of freshly squeezed lime juice

Shake all ingredients thoroughly in a cocktail shaker with

cracked ice. Strain into a chilled cocktail glass. Garnish with

pared orange peel and serve straight up.

CRANKISS

INGREDIENTS

1 part Finlandia Cranberry
(cranberry-flavored vodka)
1 dash of freshly squeezed lime juice
1 dash of cranberry cordial
Champagne, to top
1 lime twist and cranberries,
to garnish

Build all of the ingredients in a champagne flute, stir, and garnish with the lime twist and cranberries.

LIMONCELLO ITALIANO

INGREDIENTS

2 parts vodka or citron vodka
(see Tip)
½ part lemon juice
½ part sugar syrup
7-up, to top

Shake the vodka, lemon juice, and syrup in a cocktail shaker with cracked ice. Strain into a highball glass half-filled with crushed ice and a long curled length of lemon peel. Top with 7-up.

TIP

Make your own citron vodka by steeping pared rind from 6 lemons with 4oz/100g sugar in 24fl oz vodka, in a large jar. Shake the jar daily for 3–4 weeks. Once flavoring is complete, strain the vodka back into the vodka bottle. Serve citron vodka as in this recipe, or keep the bottle in the freezer and serve it neat in iced shot glasses.

GIN

CLOVER CLUB

INGREDIENTS

2 parts gin

1 part grenadine

1 egg white

1–2 teaspoons freshly squeezed
    lime juice

2 lime spirals, to garnish

Shake ingredients in a cocktail shaker with cracked ice. Strain into a

chilled cocktail glass and serve straight up with 2 spirals of lime.

PARADISE MARTINI

INGREDIENTS

2 parts gin

1½ parts freshly squeezed
    orange juice

½ part apricot brandy

4 drops of orange bitters

1 flamed orange twist

Shake all of the ingredients with ice and then double strain

into a chilled martini glass. Flame the orange twist over the drink's

surface and drop it in.

TIP

A flamed orange twist never fails to impress. Cut a small oval of peel from an orange, leaving a little pith intact. Pinch the oval skin-side out holding it over a flame. Squeeze it firmly so that the zest oil is released. The zest oil will then ignite to give you an impressive flame, with a fantastic aroma.

PARK AVENUE

INGREDIENTS

1½ parts gin

1 part sweet vermouth

1 dash of pineapple juice

Stir all of the ingredients in a mixing glass with ice until thoroughly chilled. Strain into a chilled martini glass and serve immediately.

KIWI KRAZE

INGREDIENTS

3 parts kiwi fruit juice

1 part gin

Dash of absinthe

Tonic water

Kiwi slices, to garnish

Shake the kiwi juice, gin, and a good dash of absinthe in a cocktail shaker with cracked ice. Strain into an old-fashioned glass half-filled with crushed ice. Top up with tonic water. Garnish with a slice of kiwi fruit.

BUMBLE BEE

INGREDIENTS

1 teaspoon liquid honey
1 dash of freshly squeezed lemon
    juice
2 parts gin
2 lemon slices, to garnish

Fill an old-fashioned glass with crushed ice and add the honey and lemon juice. Stir while slowly adding gin and top with more crushed ice. Garnish with lemon slices and serve with short straws.

SLOE GIN & TONIC

INGREDIENTS

1 part gin
1 part good sloe gin
1 part freshly squeezed lime juice
$\frac{1}{2}$ part sugar syrup
Tonic water, to top

Shake the gins, lime juice, and sugar syrup in a cocktail shaker with cracked ice and strain into an ice-filled highball glass. Top up with tonic water and serve with a wedge of lime.

COQ ROUGE

INGREDIENTS

2 parts light rum

1 part gin

1 part freshly squeezed lemon or
   lime juice

1 part Cointreau or triple sec

1 orange spiral, to garnish

Stir or shake with cracked ice. Strain into a chilled cocktail glass

and serve straight up. Garnish with a spiral of orange peel.

ARTHUR TOMPKINS

INGREDIENTS

2 parts gin

½ part Grand Marnier

1 dash of freshly squeezed lemon juice

1 lemon twist, to garnish

Shake the gin, Grand Marnier, and lemon juice briefly with ice and strain into an old-fashioned glass over ice.

Garnish with a twist of lemon and serve with short straws.

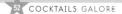
GREENBACK

INGREDIENTS

1½ parts gin

1 part green crème de menthe

1 part freshly squeezed lemon juice

Lemon slices and spirals, to garnish

Shake all of the ingredients briefly with ice and strain into an

old-fashioned glass over ice. Garnish with lemon slices and spirals.

TRIVIA

*Originally used for medicinal
purposes, it is thought that gin was first
produced in Holland in the 17th century. It was in
the 1920s, "the Cocktail Age," that gin began to be
drunk by high society, most commonly enjoyed with
tonic and a wedge of lime, or in a martini. It is widely
regarded as one of the most essential beverages to stock
for those entertaining at home. The name "gin" was
taken from the French word from juniper,
"genièvre," as juniper is one of many flavors
that is added to the spirit.*

RASPBERRY CRUSH

INGREDIENTS

15 fresh raspberries
1 part gin
1 part framboise (raspberry liqueur)
    or sugar syrup
Dash of freshly squeezed lemon juice
Club soda, to top
Extra raspberries and mint leaves,
    to garnish

Combine the fruit, gin, framboise or sugar syrup, and lemon

juice with half a glass of crushed ice in a blender. Blend until

puréed. Pour into an old-fashioned glass, and add a little club soda to top

up the glass. Garnish with raspberries and mint leaves.

DUBONNET COCKTAIL

INGREDIENTS

1 part gin
1 part Dubonnet rouge
Lemon twist, to garnish

Shake ingredients vigorously in a cocktail shaker with cracked ice.

Serve either straight up or on the rocks in an old-fashioned glass.

Garnish with a twist of lemon peel.

TIP

*Particularly popular in the
1950s, Dubonnet rouge is a
French aperitif made from
red wine flavored with quinine
and bitter herbs. If you prefer
a drier cocktail, just add
more gin.*

GIBSON MARTINI

INGREDIENTS

½ part extra dry vermouth
2 parts gin
4 pearl onions

Stir the vermouth with ice in a mixing glass then strain away any excess liquid so just the coated ice remains. Add the gin and stir until thoroughly chilled. Strain the mix into a chilled martini glass and garnish with the onions on a swizzle stick. Garnished with an olive or lemon twist instead this will become a Dry Martini (see page 57).

BRONX

INGREDIENTS

2 parts gin
2 parts dry vermouth
1 part sweet vermouth
⅓ part orange juice
1 orange spiral, to garnish

Shake ingredients vigorously in a cocktail shaker with cracked ice. Strain into a chilled cocktail glass and serve straight up with a spiral of orange peel.

ORANGE BLOSSOM

INGREDIENTS
1 part gin
1 part orange juice
Orange slices, to garnish

Shake ingredients vigorously in a cocktail shaker with cracked ice.

Strain into a chilled old-fashioned glass and serve straight up.

Garnish with a slice of orange.

OPAL MARTINI

INGREDIENTS
2 parts gin
1 part triple sec or Cointreau
2 parts freshly squeezed orange juice
1 flamed orange twist, to garnish

Shake all of the ingredients with ice and strain into

a chilled martini glass. Garnish with a flamed orange twist.

TRIVIA
Widely regarded as the original "Neo-tini," the Opal Martini was originally designed to mask the flavor of ropey gin in the Prohibition era. It remains a wonderfully balanced— and very potent—drink, despite its insalubrious beginnings.

AVIATION

INGREDIENTS

1½ parts gin
2 dashes of maraschino cherry liqueur
1 part freshly squeezed lemon juice
1 cocktail cherry, to garnish

Shake first three ingredients with ice and strain into a chilled martini glass. Garnish with a single cocktail cherry.

DRY MARTINI

INGREDIENTS

4 parts gin
1 part dry vermouth
1 pitted green olive, to garnish

Stir ingredients with cracked ice in a mixing glass. Strain into a chilled cocktail glass and serve straight up. Garnish with a pitted green olive.

"Why don't you get out of that wet coat and into a dry martini?"
Charles Butterworth,
Every Day's A Holiday

RASPBERRY COLLINS

INGREDIENTS

2 parts gin

1$^1/_2$ parts raspberry purée

$^1/_2$ part freshly squeezed lemon juice

$^1/_2$ part framboise (raspberry liqueur)

1 dash of sugar syrup

1 dash of orange bitters

Soda water, to top

2 raspberries and 1 lemon slice,
   to garnish

Shake the first six ingredients with ice and strain into a highball glass filled with crushed ice. Top with soda water and stir. Garnish with raspberries and a lemon slice.

GIMLET

INGREDIENTS

2 parts gin

1 part lime cordial

$^1/_2$ part water (optional)

1 lime wedge

Stir all of the liquid ingredients with ice until thoroughly chilled and strain into a chilled martini glass. Squeeze the lime wedge over the drink and drop in.

TRIVIA

The Gimlet was immortalized by Raymond Chandler's The Long Goodbye. *British sailors wanting to avoid scurvy took vitamin C in the form of Roses' lime cordial (hence the British epithet, Limeys). The sailors mixed the lime cordial with their daily ration of rum, and the rum barrel was tapped with a sharp little tool called a gimlet.*

MAXIM

INGREDIENTS

1¹⁄₂ parts gin

1 part dry vermouth

1 dash white crème de cacao

1 cocktail cherry, to garnish

Shake all of the ingredients with ice until thoroughly chilled, then strain

into a chilled martini glass. Garnish with a cocktail cherry.

ALEXANDER'S SISTER

INGREDIENTS

1¹⁄₂ parts gin

1 part green crème de menthe

1 part light cream

Grated nutmeg, to garnish

Shake all of the liquid ingredients with ice and strain into a chilled

martini glass. Finish with a sprinkle of grated nutmeg.

TOM COLLINS

INGREDIENTS

2 parts gin
1 part freshly squeezed lemon juice
1 part sugar syrup
Club soda, to top
Mint leaves, to garnish

Shake ingredients thoroughly in a cocktail shaker with cracked ice.

Strain into a Collins glass. Add ice cubes and fill the glass with club

soda. Garnish with mint leaves.

TRIVIA

This classic was originally made with "Old Tom" Gin. Legend has it that in 1738, a certain Captain Dudley Bradstreet of London took advantage of a legal loophole in the prohibitionist 1736 Gin Act—he hung up a sign in the shape of a tom cat and customers could purchase a measure of gin dispensed from the cat's paw.

SINGAPORE SLING

INGREDIENTS

2 parts gin
1 part cherry brandy
$\frac{1}{2}$ part freshly squeezed lemon juice
Dash of Benedictine
Dash of Cointreau or triple sec
Club soda, to top
Orange and lemon slices, and a
    maraschino cherry, to garnish

Shake the gin, cherry brandy, lemon, Benedictine, and Cointreau in a
cocktail shaker with cracked ice. Strain into a chilled Collins glass. Add ice
cubes and club soda to fill the glass. Garnish with orange and lemon slices
and a maraschino cherry.

TRIVIA
*Created by the barman at
Singapore's Raffles Hotel in
1915, the Singapore Sling saw a
revival during the '50s due to
the fascination with South
Seas' umbrella drinks.*

GIN GEENIE

INGREDIENTS

6 mint leaves

$\frac{1}{2}$ part freshly squeezed lemon juice

1 dash of sugar syrup

2 parts gin

1 mint sprig, to garnish

Muddle the mint leaves, lemon juice, and sugar syrup in the bottom of an old-fashioned glass. Fill with crushed

ice and stir. Slowly add the gin and stir again. Garnish with a sprig of mint and serve with straws.

INVITATION ONLY

INGREDIENTS

3 parts gin

$\frac{1}{2}$ part sugar syrup

$\frac{1}{2}$ part freshly squeezed lime juice

1 egg white

1 dash of crème de mûre
   (blackberry liqueur)

2 blackberries, to garnish

TIP

Don't ignore those liqueurs hanging around at the back of your drinks cupboard. Crème de mûre is a French blackberry liqueur which works fantastically well with the flavor of gin.

Shake and strain the first four ingredients over ice into a highball glass.

Lace the drink with crème de mûre and garnish with two blackberries.

BREAKFAST MARTINI

INGREDIENTS

1 teaspoon orange marmalade

2 parts gin

1 dash of freshly squeezed lemon juice

½ part triple sec

3 small triangles of toast spread with
   butter and marmalade, to garnish

Stir the marmalade with the gin in a shaker until dissolved, then add the lemon juice and triple sec. Shake until

thoroughly chilled. Strain into a chilled martini glass and garnish with the toast slices. • • • ➜

GIN SOUR

INGREDIENTS

2 parts gin

2 parts freshly squeezed orange juice

1 part freshly squeezed lemon juice

1 part egg white

½ part sugar syrup

1 lemon wedge, to garnish

TRIVIA

*The Sour was
invented as early as the
1850s, starting with the
Brandy Sour. Sours owe their
names to the small amount of
sweetener and relatively
large amount of fresh
lemon juice.*

Shake all of the liquid ingredients with ice and strain into an ice-filled

highball glass. Garnish with a lemon wedge and serve with straws.

ARIZONA COOLER

INGREDIENTS

4 parts cranberry juice
2 parts gin
2 parts grapefruit juice
Lime wedges, to garnish

Fill a highball glass with ice and add the cranberry juice. Shake the gin
and grapefruit juice with ice and strain over the cranberry juice to create
a "floating" effect. Garnish with lime wedges and serve with straws.

HEDGEROW SLING

INGREDIENTS

2 parts sloe gin
1 part freshly squeezed lemon juice
1 dash of sugar syrup
Soda water, to top
½ measure crème de mûre
    (blackberry liqueur)
2 blueberries, 2 blackberries and
    1 lemon slice, to garnish

Shake the gin, lemon juice, and sugar syrup with ice, and strain into an
ice-filled highball glass. Top with soda water and lace with the crème de
mûre. Garnish with blueberries, blackberries, and a lemon slice.

ALEXANDER

INGREDIENTS

2 parts gin
1 part crème de cacao
1 part heavy cream

Shake the ingredients vigorously in a cocktail shaker with cracked ice.

Strain into a chilled cocktail glass and serve straight up. For the finishing

touch, sprinkle with a fine dusting of cocoa.

MAIDEN'S BLUSH

INGREDIENTS

1½ parts gin
½ part triple sec
1 dash of grenadine
1 dash of freshly squeezed lemon juice
Lemon slices, to garnish

Shake all of the liquid ingredients with ice and strain into

an ice-filled old-fashioned glass. Garnish with lemon slices

and serve with short straws.

TRIVIA

*There are three main
styles of gin. London Dry Gin,
which, despite its name, can be
made anywhere in the world;
Plymouth Gin, which can only be made
in Plymouth, England because of the soft
water available in the region; and Old
Tom Gin, a sweet style, which was
once the most popular but is
now almost obsolete.*

RUM

CUBAN PEACH

INGREDIENTS

1 part peach brandy
1 part white Cuban rum
1 teaspoon freshly squeezed
   lime juice
Pinch of sugar

Shake all ingredients thoroughly in a cocktail shaker with cracked ice.
Strain into a cocktail glass half-filled with crushed ice. Float two thin
slices of peach and a sprig of mint on the top to garnish.

CANCHANCHARA

INGREDIENTS

1 part liquid honey
2 parts white rum
1 part freshly squeezed lime juice
1 dash soda water
1 lime wedge, to garnish

In a heavy-based old-fashioned glass, stir the honey, rum, and lime juice
until the honey has dissolved. Then add ice, stir again, and garnish with a
lime wedge. Serve with a stirrer.

FESTIVE FLARE

INGREDIENTS

2 tablespoons brown sugar

2 tablespoons water

2 tablespoons orange juice

Small piece of cinnamon stick

1 star anise

5fl oz US/160ml red wine

1 tablespoon golden or dark rum

TRIVIA

There's a taste of the West Indies in every sip of rum thanks to one thing—molasses. Nearly all rum is made from this dark, sweet syrup which is a bi-product of sugar cane. Water is added and a special yeast joins the mix to aid fermentation. Then each rum distillery will add its own unique flavorings according to its closely-guarded recipe.

Put the sugar, water, orange juice, piece of cinnamon stick and star anise into a small pan and heat gently until the sugar dissolves, then bring almost to the boil. Leave off the heat for 10 minutes to allow the flavors to infuse. Add the wine to the pan and warm it through. Remove the cinnamon stick and pour into a warmed toddy glass. Measure the rum into a small soup ladle, warm the ladle over the gas flame, gently shaking it until hot vapors ignite the rum. Carefully pour the flaming rum into the glass of warm wine. Let the flames die down and the top of the glass cool before you drink it.

ACAPULCO GOLD

INGREDIENTS

2 parts pineapple juice
1 part grapefruit juice
1 part tequila
1 part golden rum
1 part coconut milk

Combine all the ingredients in a cocktail shaker with cracked ice. Shake well. Strain into a Boston glass half-filled with ice cubes. Decorate with a fun straw and a monkey in a palm tree.

AUSTIN POWERS

INGREDIENTS

3 parts clear apple juice
1 part spiced golden rum
$\frac{1}{2}$ part Amaretto
$\frac{1}{2}$ part blue curaçao
$\frac{1}{2}$ part freshly squeezed lime juice

Shake all ingredients thoroughly in a cocktail shaker with cracked ice. Strain into a Boston or highball glass half-filled with ice. Garnish with slices of orange, starfruit, strawberry, and a maraschino cherry. Serve with straws and a parasol.

ALMOND BREEZE

INGREDIENTS

1 part white rum
$\frac{1}{2}$ part of Amaretto or orgeat
$\frac{1}{2}$ part melon liqueur
Tonic water, to top

Shake the rum and liqueurs in a cocktail shaker with cracked ice. Strain

into a highball glass, half-filled with crushed ice. Top with tonic water.

TRIVIA

*Rum is said to date back
to the early 16th century. At first
it was a rough spirit that colonists drank,
but its popularity later spread to Western
Europe and then throughout the rest of the
world. Rum is made from the sweet juice of sugar
cane, however, some distilleries use molasses
instead. In the present day, it is most common for
all rum to be aged in used oak barrels from
anywhere between one to thirty years. There
are two types of rum, light and dark, the
latter being a result of longer aging
and the addition of caramel.*

MOJITO

INGREDIENTS

8 mint leaves

1/2 lime

2 dashes sugar syrup

2 parts white rum

1 dash soda water

1 sprig of mint, to garnish

TRIVIA

"Muddling" is the term used for the process by which a fruit or herb is crushed to release its flavors. The cocktail maker uses a blunt-ended tool called a muddler, which is similar to a pestle.

In the base of a highball glass, muddle the mint, lime, and sugar syrup.

Fill the glass with crushed ice and add the rum. Stir, then add a dash of

soda water. Garnish with a mint sprig and serve with long straws.

HONEYSUCKLE

INGREDIENTS

1 part Creole Shrub Rum

1 part gold rum

1/2 part freshly squeezed lime juice

1/2 part liquid orange blossom honey

4 drops orange bitters

1 flamed orange twist, to garnish

Shake all of the ingredients with ice and strain into a chilled martini

glass. Garnish with a flamed orange twist.

HAVANA COCKTAIL

INGREDIENTS

1 part cream sherry
1 part golden rum
1 teaspoon freshly squeezed lemon
   or lime juice
Lemon or lime spirals

Shake the ingredients thoroughly in a cocktail shaker with cracked ice.

Strain into a cocktail glass. Garnish with a lemon or lime peel spiral.

MAI TAI

INGREDIENTS

1 part light rum
½ part dark rum
1 part orange juice
1 part apricot brandy
½ part tequila
½ part Cointreau or triple sec
2 dashes of grenadine
Dash of Amaretto or orgeat
Dash of Angostura bitters

Shake ingredients vigorously in a cocktail shaker with cracked ice. Strain into an old-fashioned glass or large goblet, half-filled with crushed ice. Decorate with slices of orange, lemon, and lime, a maraschino cherry, and a sprig of mint.

KNICKERBOCKER

INGREDIENTS

5 parts light rum

1 part freshly squeezed lemon juice

1 part raspberry syrup

1 part pineapple syrup

Orange spirals and a maraschino
   cherry, to garnish

Shake ingredients thoroughly in a cocktail shaker with cracked ice. Strain

into a chilled cocktail glass and serve straight up. Garnish with spirals of

orange peel and a maraschino cherry.

TRE

INGREDIENTS

2 parts gold rum

1 part freshly pressed apple juice

2 dashes Chambord (black
   raspberry liqueur)

1 dash sugar syrup

1 lime twist, to garnish

TRIVIA

*Chambord is a
French liqueur made from
honey and black raspberries.
The raspberries are hand-picked
and then mellowed in oak barrels.
The distinctive and royal-looking
orb-shaped bottle with its brass
decoration is a must-have in
any cocktail bar.*

Add all of the ingredients to a mixing glass, then fill with ice. Stir to chill

thoroughly, then strain into a frozen martini glass. Adjust the sweetness

by taste. Garnish with a lime twist.

BACARDI

INGREDIENTS

2 parts light Bacardi rum
1 part freshly squeezed lemon or
  lime juice
1 part grenadine

Shake ingredients thoroughly in a cocktail shaker with cracked ice. Strain

into a chilled old-fashioned glass and serve straight up. Garnish with a

slice of lemon and a maraschino cherry.

WEST INDIAN ICED TEA

INGREDIENTS

1 part Bacardi Oro (gold rum)
½ part Grand Marnier
1 part freshly squeezed orange juice
4 mint leaves
4 parts freshly brewed English
  Breakfast tea
1 orange slice and 1 mint sprig,
  to garnish

Shake all of the ingredients (including mint leaves—not sprig) with ice, and strain into an ice-filled highball

glass. Garnish with an orange slice and mint sprig, and serve with straws, in the sun.

BANANA DAIQUIRI

INGREDIENTS

1 small banana, peeled and sliced
1 part white rum
1 part golden rum
½ part crème de banane
½ part freshly squeezed lime juice
½ part coconut milk
1 teaspoon sugar syrup

Blend all ingredients with crushed ice until smooth. Pour into a large, chilled Boston glass. Add a few ice cubes. Garnish with a large twist of banana leaf. Banana leaves are available from good supermarkets.

PRESIDENTE

INGREDIENTS

2 parts white rum
½ part dry vermouth
½ part sweet vermouth
1 dash triple sec
1 orange twist

Stir all of the liquid ingredients in a mixing glass with ice until thoroughly chilled. Strain into a chilled martini glass, squeeze the orange twist over the drink, and drop in.

TIP

Many cocktail recipes ask you to "stir with ice and strain," but what's the best way of doing this without making a mess? Firstly, pour the ingredients into a mixing glass and then add the ice. Use a long bar spoon (ideally with a twisted handle) and gently stir the drink until thoroughly chilled. Then use a Hawthorne strainer to strain the drink into the glass, usually a chilled martini glass.

STRAWBERRY DAIQUIRI

INGREDIENTS

2 parts white rum

½ part strawberry liqueur

1 part freshly squeezed lime juice

1 dash strawberry syrup

4 ripe strawberries

1 split strawberry, to garnish

Blend all of the ingredients with a small scoop of crushed ice
and pour into a martini glass. Garnish with a split
strawberry on the rim of the glass.

TRIVIA

*Daiquiris are any cocktails whose main
ingredients are rum and lime juice. There are
many versions, but those that gained international
fame are the ones made in the famous Floridita bar in
Havana. Daiquiri is also the name of a beach near Santiago,
Cuba, and an iron mine in that area. It is believed that the
cocktail was invented by an American named Jennings Cox, an
engineer who worked in that very mine. When Cox ran out of gin
while entertaining American guests, he added lime juice and
sugar to improve the taste of the local rum. In 1909, Admiral
Lucius W. Johnson, a US Navy medical officer, tried Cox's
drink and introduced it to the Army and Navy Club in
Washington DC. Ernest Hemingway made daiquiris
particularly famous, drinking them regularly
in Havana while writing* For Whom
the Bell Tolls.

PIÑA COLADA

INGREDIENTS

2 parts golden, white, or dark rum

3 parts pineapple juice or ¹/₂ cup
  diced pineapple pieces

1 part coconut cream or fresh
  coconut milk

¹/₂ part light cream

2 dashes of Angostura bitters
  (optional)

Combine all ingredients with four or five ice cubes in a blender. Blend

until smooth. Pour into a large goblet or Boston glass. Garnish with a

large wedge of pineapple and a maraschino cherry.

MIAMI

INGREDIENTS

5 parts light rum

2 parts freshly squeezed lemon juice

2 parts white crème de menthe

Orange twist

Shake thoroughly in a cocktail shaker with cracked ice.

Strain into a chilled cocktail glass and serve straight up. Garnish with a

twist of orange peel.

CUBA LIBRE

INGREDIENTS

2 parts white rum
½ lime
Cola, to top

Add the rum to an ice-filled highball glass. Cut the lime into four segments and squeeze into the drink, dropping each one in. Top with cola, stir, and serve with straws.

TRIVIA
The Cuba Libre was allegedly invented by American soldiers who combined a new soft drink called Coca Cola with the local rum and a squeeze of fresh lime. Most importantly, the lime squeeze is what sets a Cuba Libre apart from a rum-and-cola.

HAVANA BEACH

INGREDIENTS

2 parts golden or white Cuban rum
3 parts pineapple juice
1 teaspoon sugar syrup
Ginger ale, to top

Shake the rum, pineapple juice, and syrup vigorously in a cocktail shaker with cracked ice. Strain into an old-fashioned glass, half-filled with ice cubes. Top with ginger ale. Garnish with a few pineapple cubes.

WHITE WITCH

INGREDIENTS

1 part white rum
1/2 part white crème de cacao
   (chocolate-flavored liqueur)
1/2 part Cointreau
1 dash freshly squeezed lime juice
   soda water, to top
1 lime wedge and 1 orange wedge,
   to garnish

Shake the rum, crème de cacao, Cointreau, and lime juice together and strain into an ice-filled old-fashioned glass. Top with soda and stir. Garnish with lime and orange wedges.

BLACK WIDOW

INGREDIENTS

1 1/2 parts dark rum
1 part Southern Comfort
1/2 part freshly squeezed lime juice
2 dashes sugar syrup
4 drops Angostura bitters
1 lime wedge, to garnish

Shake all of the ingredients with ice and strain into a chilled martini glass. Garnish with a wedge of lime on the rim of the glass.

WINDWARD ISLAND

INGREDIENTS
1 part golden rum
½ part Tia Maria
Cola, to top

Shake the rum and Tia Maria vigorously in a cocktail shaker with cracked ice. Strain into an old-fashioned glass almost filled with ice cubes. Top with cola and garnish with orange slices.

ZOMBIE

INGREDIENTS
1 part dark rum
1 part light rum
1 part golden rum
½ part apricot brandy
½ part curaçao
2 parts orange juice

2 parts pineapple juice
½ part grenadine syrup
1 part freshly squeezed lime juice
Long orange spiral

Shake all the ingredients vigorously in a cocktail shaker with cracked ice. Strain into an ice-filled Boston glass. Float ½ part overproof rum on top. (Overproof or high strength rum is any rum with over 57% alcohol per volume.) Garnish with a long spiral of orange.

GRENADA

INGREDIENTS

2 parts gold rum
1 part freshly squeezed orange juice
½ part sweet vermouth
Ground cinnamon

Shake all of the liquid ingredients with ice and strain into a chilled martini glass. Sprinkle the ground cinnamon through a flame and on to the surface of the drink.

PLANTERS' PUNCH

INGREDIENTS

3 parts dark Jamaican rum
1 part freshly squeezed lime juice
1 teaspoon sugar
Dash of Angostura bitters
Club soda

Shake the rum, lime juice, sugar, and bitters in a cocktail shaker with cracked ice. Strain into a highball glass half-filled with crushed ice. Add club soda to fill. Garnish with a maraschino cherry, a cube of pineapple, a slice of orange, and a sprig of mint.

TEQUILA

MARGARITA

INGREDIENTS

2 parts tequila
1 part Cointreau or triple sec
½ part freshly squeezed lime juice
1 lime wedge, to garnish

Rub round the rim of a chilled cocktail or margarita glass with a wedge of lime, then dip into fine salt. Shake the ingredients vigorously in a cocktail shaker with cracked ice. Strain into the glass. Serve straight up garnished with a wedge of lime.

FROZEN STRAWBERRY MARGARITA

INGREDIENTS

4 ripe strawberries
1 part gold tequila
1 part freshly squeezed lime juice
½ part Cointreau
½ part strawberry liqueur
1 split strawberry, to garnish

Blend all of the ingredients with a small scoop of crushed ice. Serve in a large coupette garnished with a split strawberry on the rim.

TIP
Whenever you dip the rim of your margarita glass in the fine sea salt, always wipe the inner rim to make sure there is no salt on this surface as it will taint the drink.

PASSION FRUIT MARGARITA

INGREDIENTS

1½ parts gold tequila

1 part freshly squeezed lime juice

½ part passion fruit syrup

1 part Cointreau

1 passion fruit, flesh only

1 lime wedge, to garnish

Shake all ingredients with ice and strain into a coupette.

Garnish with a lime wedge on the rim.

TRIVIA

The Margarita's origins, like those of all classic cocktails, are shrouded in legend. Its native home, like that of the spirit tequila, is believed to be Mexico. Tales tell of a beautiful woman named Margarita, thwarted love, and a bartender who created a drink in her memory.

TIJUANA SLING

INGREDIENTS

1¹⁄₂ parts gold tequila
¹⁄₂ part crème de cassis
  (black currant liqueur)
¹⁄₂ part freshly squeezed lime juice
2 drops of Peychaud's bitters
Ginger ale, to top
1 lime slice and blueberries,
  to garnish

Pour the tequila, crème de cassis, lime juice, and bitters into a shaker and shake with ice. Strain this into an

ice-filled sling glass, top with ginger ale, and garnish with the lime slice and blueberries. Serve with straws.

MEXICAN WAVE

INGREDIENTS

1 part tequila
¹⁄₂ part crème de cassis
  (black currant liqueur)
¹⁄₂ part sugar syrup
Ginger ale, to top
Lime slices, to garnish

Shake the tequila, crème de cassis, and sugar syrup in a cocktail shaker

with cracked ice. Strain into an old-fashioned glass, top with ginger ale,

and mix with a glass swizzle stick. Float a few thin lime slices

on top to garnish.

TEQUILA SUNRISE

INGREDIENTS

2 parts tequila
5 parts orange juice
½ part grenadine
1 orange slice and 1 maraschino
  cherry, to garnish

Pour the tequila and orange juice into a highball glass filled with ice. Stir.

When it settles, pour the grenadine in a circle around the top of the drink

and let it fall to the bottom. Garnish with a slice of orange and a

maraschino cherry.

TRIVIA

The Tequila Sunrise may have originated at the Agua Caliente racetrack in Mexico in Prohibition times, when Californians drove across the border to take part in the races and enjoy legal hits of liquor.

THIGH HIGH

INGREDIENTS

1 part gold tequila
1 part dark crème de cacao
1 part light cream
3 strawberries
1 dash of strawberry syrup
1 split strawberry, to garnish

Blend all of the ingredients with a small scoop of crushed ice and serve in a hurricane glass. Place the strawberry on the rim of the glass as a garnish.

BAJA SOUR

INGREDIENTS

1½ parts gold tequila
2 drops of orange bitters
1 part lemon juice
½ part sugar syrup
½ egg white
1 dash of dry sherry
Lemon slices, to garnish

Shake all of the ingredients, except the sherry, with ice and strain into an ice-filled old-fashioned glass. Drizzle over the sherry and garnish with slices of lemon.

TEQUINI

INGREDIENTS

3 parts silver tequila

3 drops of orange bitters

½ part dry vermouth

2 black olives, to garnish

Pour all of the ingredients into a mixing glass, add ice, and stir until thoroughly chilled. Strain into a frozen martini glass and garnish with two black olives on a swizzle stick.

FOREST FRUIT

INGREDIENTS

1 lime wedge

Fine brown sugar

2 blackberries

2 raspberries

2 teaspoons Chambord
  (black raspberry liqueur)

2 teaspoons crème de mûre
  (blackberry liqueur)

1½ parts silver tequila

½ part Cointreau

1 part freshly squeezed lemon juice

Lemon slices, to garnish

TRIVIA

Cointreau was first established in 1849 in Angers, France by confectioner Adolphe Cointreau and his brother Edouard-Jean. The Cointreau we know today was created by Edouard Cointreau (son of Edouard-Jean) and first marketed around the world from the 1870s. It is made to a unique secret recipe using bitter and sweet orange peels shipped to France from around the world which are macerated in alcohol for several weeks to bring out the citrus flavors and aromas.

Moisten the rim of a large old-fashioned glass with the lime wedge and coat with brown sugar. In the glass, muddle the fresh berries with the Chambord and crème de mûre. Fill the glass with crushed ice. Now, add the tequila, Cointreau, and lemon juice. Stir to mix thoroughly, garnish with lemon slices, and serve with straws.

BORDER CROSSING

INGREDIENTS

1¹⁄₂ parts gold tequila

1 part freshly squeezed lime juice

1 part liquid honey

4 drops of orange bitters

Bitter lemon, to top

Lemon slices, to garnish

Shake the first four ingredients with ice and strain into a sling glass. Top with bitter lemon, stir, and garnish with

lemon slices. Serve with long straws.

SOUR APPLE

INGREDIENTS

1¹⁄₂ parts gold tequila

2 dashes Cointreau

¹⁄₂ part apple schnapps

¹⁄₂ part freshly squeezed lime juice

1 part freshly pressed apple juice

1 apple sliver, to garnish

Shake all ingredients with ice and strain into a chilled martini glass.

Garnish with the sliver of apple floating on the drink.

DESPERADO

INGREDIENTS

½ lime, cut into segments
1 tablespoon brown sugar
Dark beer, to top
1 part gold tequila

Muddle the lime and sugar in the base of a large highball glass. Fill with

ice and slowly pour the beer and tequila over. Stir, and serve.

OFF-SHORE

INGREDIENTS

1 part gold tequila
1 part white rum
6 mint leaves
3 chunks fresh pineapple
2 parts pineapple juice
1 part light cream
1 mint sprig, to garnish

Blend all of the ingredients with a small scoop of crushed ice and serve in

a hurricane glass. Garnish with a mint sprig and serve with straws.

KALASHNIKOV

INGREDIENTS

1 orange slice

Superfine sugar

Ground coffee

1 part gold tequila

Dip the orange slice in fine white sugar and then sprinkle ground coffee

over it. Instruct the drinker to suck the flavored orange, drink the shot,

then bite the orange.

TEQUILA SLAMMER

INGREDIENTS

1 dash of dark crème de cacao

1 part champagne

1 part gold tequila

Pour all of the ingredients into a heavy-based

old-fashioned glass. Instruct the drinker to cover the

glass with their hand, bang the glass on a hard surface,

and down the contents in one.

TRIVIA

The intoxicating
power of "slammers" comes
from the fact that the alcohol
dissolves in the bubbles created by
the shock of slamming the glass
down, and so is absorbed into the
blood stream much more quickly.
Slammers can be made using
any kind of fizzy mixer.

EASY TIGER

INGREDIENTS

2 parts gold tequila

1 part freshly squeezed lime juice

2 teaspoons liquid honey

2 teaspoons ginger cordial

1 orange twist, to garnish

Add all of the ingredients to a mixing glass and stir until the honey has

dissolved. Then add ice, shake, and strain into a chilled champagne flute.

Garnish with an orange twist.

TRIVIA

Tequila is made from
the heart of the blue agave
plant, a member of the lily family—not
a cactus as commonly thought—and has
become Mexico's National treasure. At
present, there are over 500 types of tequila
available to the consumer. A common
misconception is that high quality tequilas and
mescals have a worm in the bottle. This is not
the case however, as high quality tequila
would never have such an addition—it
was just an American marketing
ploy introduced in the
1940s!

WHISKEY

RUSTY NAIL

INGREDIENTS

2 parts Scotch

1 part Drambuie

1 long lemon spiral, to garnish

Combine ingredients with ice in a mixing glass and stir.

Strain into an old-fashioned glass filled with ice. Garnish with

a long spiral of lemon rind.

WHISKY MAC

INGREDIENTS

2 parts Scotch whisky

1½ parts ginger wine

Pour both ingredients over ice in an old-fashioned

glass and stir to mix.

TRIVIA

*Many different types
of whiskey exist, including
Scotch, Irish, Rye, Canadian,
Japanese, and Bourbon. It is a barrel-
aged, distilled spirit, produced from grain
or malt. Scotch can only be so-named if it is
made in Scotland. Bourbon is named after
Bourbon County, Kentucky, where it
originated. The name whiskey derives
originally from the Gaelic "uisge
beatha," meaning "water
of life."*

FRISCO

INGREDIENTS

2 parts rye

1 part Benedictine

½ part freshly squeezed lemon juice

1 lemon twist, to garnish

Shake ingredients thoroughly in a cocktail shaker with cracked ice. Strain into a chilled cocktail glass and serve

straight up. Garnish with a twist of lemon peel.

MILLIONAIRE

INGREDIENTS

3 parts bourbon

1 part curaçao

1 egg white

½ part grenadine

1 orange slice, to garnish

Stir ingredients well in a mixing glass with cracked ice. Strain into a

chilled cocktail glass and serve straight up. Garnish with a slice of orange.

CHIN CHIN

INGREDIENTS

1 part Scotch whisky
½ part liquid honey
½ part freshly pressed apple juice
Champagne, to top

Shake first three ingredients with ice and strain into a chilled flute. Top

with champagne and stir before serving.

MANHATTAN

INGREDIENTS

2 parts rye
1 part dry vermouth
1 part sweet vermouth
Dash of Angostura bitters
1 lemon slice, to garnish

Stir ingredients in a mixing glass with cracked ice. Strain into a cocktail

glass and serve straight up. Garnish with a slice of lemon.

OLD-FASHIONED

INGREDIENTS

½ teaspoon sugar

2 dashes of Angostura bitters

1 teaspoon water

1½ parts rye

1 orange slice, 1 pineapple slice,
   and 1 maraschino cherry, to garnish

Put the sugar in an old-fashioned glass. Add the bitters and water.

Muddle to dissolve the sugar. Add the rye with an ice cube and stir

with a glass rod. Garnish with a slice of orange, a slice of pineapple,

and a maraschino cherry.

SILKY PIN

INGREDIENTS

1 part Scotch whisky

1 part Drambuie Cream

Pour the ingredients over ice in an old-fashioned glass and

serve with a stirrer.

*"So make it
another old-fashioned
please.
Leave out the cherry,
Leave out the orange,
Leave out the bitters,
Just make it a straight rye!"*
Cole Porter, Make It Another
Old-Fashioned, Please

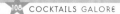

COLONEL T

INGREDIENTS

2 parts Bourbon

1 part apricot brandy

4 parts pineapple juice

1 pineapple leaf, to garnish

Shake all of the ingredients with ice and strain over ice into sling glass.

Garnish with the pineapple leaf and serve with straws.

RASPBERRY LYNCHBURG

INGREDIENTS

2 parts Jack Daniels

½ part Chambord
   (black raspberry liqueur)

1 part freshly squeezed lime juice

1 part raspberry purée

1 dash of sugar syrup

Lemonade, to top

3 raspberries, to garnish

Shake the first five ingredients together and strain over ice into a highball glass. Top with lemonade and stir.

Garnish with the raspberries and serve with straws.

SAZERAC

INGREDIENTS

1 part absinthe

Chilled water

1 part bourbon

1 part brandy

½ part sugar syrup

6 drops of Angostura bitters

6 drops of Peychaud's bitters

Fill an old-fashioned glass with ice, pour in the absinthe, fill it up with water, and set aside. Shake the remaining ingredients in a cocktail shaker with cracked ice. Discard the watery absinthe then strain the bourbon mixture into the flavored glass.

GODFATHER SOUR

INGREDIENTS

1½ parts Bourbon

1 part amaretto

1 part freshly squeezed lemon juice

1 dash of sugar syrup

1 egg white

4 drops of Angostura bitters

Lemon slices, to garnish

TRIVIA

The "Sour" is the original cocktail first mentioned in 1862 in Jerry Thomas' book "How To Mix Drinks" which also includes some long lost classics such as a "Saratoga Brace Up" and a "Philadelphia Fish House Punch."

Shake all of the ingredients with ice and strain into an ice-filled old-fashioned glass. Garnish with lemon slices and serve with straws.

RHETT BUTLER

INGREDIENTS

2 parts Bourbon

4 parts cranberry juice

2 lime wedges

Pour the ingredients over ice in an old-fashioned glass. Squeeze the limes

and drop into the drink. Serve with a stirrer.

SOLERA ECLIPSE

INGREDIENTS

2 parts single malt whiskey
   (such as Glenfiddich Solera Reserve)

1 dash of sweet vermouth

1 dash of dry vermouth

4 drops of Angostura bitters

2 cocktail cherries and a pitted green
   olive, to garnish

Shake the ingredients with ice and strain over crushed ice.

Garnish with the cherries and olive.

WHISKEY SOUR

INGREDIENTS

2 parts rye
1 part freshly squeezed lemon juice
1 teaspoon sugar
1 lemon spiral, to garnish

Shake vigorously in a cocktail shaker with cracked ice, until foamy. Pour into a chilled old-fashioned glass. Garnish with a spiral of lemon peel.

"I'm perfectly capable of fixing my own breakfast. As a matter of fact, I had two peanut butter sandwiches and two Whiskey Sours."
Tom Ewell, The Seven Year Itch

LORETTO LEMONADE

INGREDIENTS

1½ parts Bourbon
½ part Midori (melon liqueur)
½ part freshly squeezed lime juice
1 part freshly pressed apple juice
Ginger beer, to top
1 lime wedge and 1 mint sprig,
    to garnish

Shake the first four ingredients with ice and strain into an ice-filled highball glass. Top with ginger beer, stir, and garnish with the mint sprig and lime wedge. Serve with straws.

FRONTIER

INGREDIENTS

2 parts Bourbon

½ part Benedictine

2 teaspoons Vanilla Madagascar (vanilla liqueur)

2 drops of Angostura bitters

1 orange twist, to garnish

As with the Old-Fashioned (see page 107), use gradual dilution to build
and mix this drink. Garnish with the orange twist.

MINT JULEP

INGREDIENTS

1 teaspoon sugar

1 tablespoon chopped mint leaves

1 tablespoon water

1½ parts bourbon

1 small bunch of fresh mint

Put the sugar and chopped mint in a mortar and bruise the leaves with
a pestle to make a paste. Add the water and continue stirring. Fill an
old-fashioned glass half-full with crushed ice. Add the mint syrup and
bourbon. Fill the glass with more crushed ice and tuck the bunch of mint
into the ice with a couple of short straws.

MORELLO BOURBON DAIQUIRI

INGREDIENTS

2 parts Bourbon

1 part Morello cherry purée

1 part freshly squeezed lime juice

¹/₂ part sugar syrup

Lime wedges, to garnish

Shake the first four ingredients together with ice. This drink may be served either straight up in a martini glass

or on the rocks in an old-fashioned glass. Garnish with lime wedges.

FRISKY BUCK

INGREDIENTS

2 parts Bourbon

¹/₂ part butterscotch schnapps

1¹/₂ parts pineapple juice

Cocktail cherry, to garnish

Shake all of the liquid ingredients with ice and strain into a chilled martini

glass. Garnish with the cherry on a swizzle stick.

CLASSIC IRISH COFFEE

INGREDIENTS

2 parts Irish whiskey

1 teaspoon sugar

Hot filter coffee, to top

Whipped cream

Coffee beans, to garnish

Pour the coffee, sugar, and whiskey into a large wine glass. Float the

cream and garnish with coffee beans.

FIREBALL

INGREDIENTS

1 part Glayva

1 part Glenfiddich

Three-quarters fill a thin-stemmed glass with crushed ice and pour in the

Glayva and Glenfiddich together. Stir gently.

BLUE BLAZER

INGREDIENTS

1 part Scotch
1 part boiling water
1 teaspoon sugar

Combine the whiskey and the water in a pewter mug or toddy glass.
Ignite the liquid and, while it is blazing, carefully pour it back and
forth from one mug to another. If done correctly, it will look like a
continuous stream of liquid fire. Sweeten with the sugar.

KENTUCKY CREAM TEA

INGREDIENTS

2 parts Bourbon
$\frac{1}{2}$ part dark crème de cacao
1 dash of krupnik vodka
    (honey-flavored vodka)
1 dash of Cointreau
$1\frac{1}{2}$ parts heavy cream
2 cocktail cherries, to garnish

Fill a sling glass with crushed ice and build the ingredients in the above order. Float the cream on top and
garnish with cocktail cherries on a swizzle stick.

BRANDY

NICE PEAR

INGREDIENTS
1½ parts brandy
1 part Poire William (pear liqueur)
½ part sweet vermouth
Peeled pear slices, to garnish

Pour all of the liquid ingredients into a mixing glass, add ice, and stir until thoroughly chilled. Strain the mix into a frozen martini glass and garnish with slices of peeled pear.

BLUE ANGEL

INGREDIENTS
1 part blue curaçao
1 part Parfait d'amour
1 part brandy
1 part freshly squeezed lemon juice
1 part light cream
1 star fruit slice, to garnish

Shake all the ingredients in a cocktail shaker with cracked ice. Strain into a margarita or cocktail glass. Garnish with a slice of star fruit.

BETWEEN THE SHEETS

INGREDIENTS

1 part light rum
1 part brandy
1 part Cointreau or triple sec
1 part freshly squeezed lemon juice
$\frac{1}{2}$ part sugar syrup (optional)

Combine all the ingredients in a cocktail shaker with cracked ice.

Shake well. Strain into a chilled cocktail glass. Serve straight up.

TRIVIA

Brandy was introduced to Northern Europe in the 16th century by Dutch traders. The name actually originated from the Dutch word "brandewijn," meaning "burnt wine." Brandy is produced by distilling grape wines, or more generally, to spirits distilled from various fermented fruits. Fruit brandy is usually clear and colorless and should be served chilled. Even poor quality wine can make good brandy.

INCOGNITO

INGREDIENTS

1½ parts brandy
½ part dry vermouth
½ part apricot brandy
4 drops of Angostura bitters
2 ripe apricot slices, to garnish

Shake all ingredients and strain into a chilled martini glass. Garnish with two

slices of ripe apricot on the rim of the glass.

CARIBBEAN CHAMPAGNE COCKTAIL

INGREDIENTS

¼ part light rum
¼ part crème de banane
   (banana liqueur)
Dash of Angostura bitters
Chilled champagne, to top
Banana slices, maraschino cherry,
   and pineapple leaf, to garnish

Pour the rum, crème de banane, and Angostura bitters into a champagne

flute. Top with champagne and stir gently with a glass rod. Decorate with

slices of banana, a maraschino cherry, and a pineapple leaf.

PISCO SOUR

INGREDIENTS

2 parts pisco (Peruvian brandy)
1½ parts freshly squeezed lime juice
½ part sugar syrup
½ part fresh egg white
2 drops of Angostura bitters
2 cocktail cherries, to garnish

Shake all of the liquid ingredients with ice and strain over crushed ice into a large old-fashioned glass.

Garnish with two cherries on a swizzle stick.

CLASSIC COCKTAIL

INGREDIENTS

1½ parts brandy
½ part curaçao
½ part maraschino
½ part freshly squeezed lime juice
½ part sugar syrup
2 maraschino cherries, to garnish

Shake ingredients in a cocktail shaker with cracked ice. Strain into a

cocktail glass. Serve straight up and garnish with maraschino cherries.

JAFFA

INGREDIENTS

1 part brandy

1 part dark crème de cacao

½ part Mandarine Napoléon

3 drops of orange bitters

1 part light cream

Orange chocolate shavings and long
   orange spirals, to garnish

TRIVIA

*Mandarine
Napoléon is a Belgian
pure spirit infused with
the freshest Sicilian
mandarin peel and
blended with
cognac.*

Shake all of the liquid ingredients with ice and strain into a chilled martini

glass. Garnish with orange chocolate shavings and spirals of orange peel.

BRANDY FIX

INGREDIENTS

1 bar spoon confectioners' sugar

1 bar spoon water

½ part freshly squeezed lemon juice

½ part cherry brandy

1 part brandy

Lemon slices, to garnish

In the base of a short highball glass, stir the sugar and water together to dissolve. Then fill the glass with

crushed ice and add the two brandies. Garnish with slices of lemon and serve with straws.

PETITE MARTINI

INGREDIENTS

2 parts VS cognac

½ part Cointreau

1 dash of sugar syrup

4 drops of Angostura bitters

1 part pineapple juice

1 caramelized pineapple slice,
    to garnish

Shake all of the ingredients with ice and strain into a chilled martini

glass. Garnish with a slice of caramelized pineapple.

SIDECAR

INGREDIENTS

3 parts brandy

1 part Cointreau or triple sec

1 part freshly squeezed lemon juice

Lemon spiral and a maraschino cherry,
    to garnish

Shake the ingredients vigorously in a cocktail shaker with cracked ice.

Strain into a chilled cocktail glass and serve straight up with a spiral of

lemon and a maraschino cherry.

STINGER

INGREDIENTS

2 parts brandy

2 parts white crème de menthe

1 part freshly squeezed lime juice

1 lime twist, to garnish

Shake ingredients vigorously in a cocktail shaker with cracked ice. Strain

into a chilled highball glass and serve straight up with a twist of lime.

TRADITIONAL SANGRIA

INGREDIENTS

1 part Spanish brandy

4 parts red wine

4 parts lemonade

1 part freshly squeezed orange juice

Orange slices

Lemon slices

Apple slices

Cinnamon stick

Pour all of the ingredients into ice-filled highball glasses and garnish with pieces of the fruit. It is best

made in larger quantities for a group and best consumed sitting on a beautiful sandy beach! Try and make

it two hours before serving as this will give the liquid time to be infused with the fruit flavors. Just fill with

fresh ice before serving.

FRENCH 90

INGREDIENTS

1 part cognac
½ part freshly squeezed lime juice
1 dash of sugar syrup
Champagne, to top
1 lime twist, to garnish

Shake the cognac, lime juice, and sugar syrup with ice and strain into a chilled flute. Top the mix with champagne and garnish with a lime twist.

NOT TONIGHT JOSEPHINE

INGREDIENTS

3 parts red wine
1 part Napoleon brandy
Dash of Pernod
2 cocktail onions and a maraschino
    cherry, to garnish

Pour the red wine into a brandy glass with a couple of ice cubes. Add the brandy and Pernod. Stir, and garnish with cocktail onions and a maraschino cherry.

MOULIN ROUGE

INGREDIENTS
4 parts pineapple juice
½ part brandy
Champagne or sparkling wine, to top

Shake the pineapple juice and brandy thoroughly in a cocktail shaker with

cracked ice. Strain into a highball glass, half-filled with crushed ice. Top

with champagne or sparkling wine and stir.

TRIVIA
Cognac is brandy
—more specifically, fine
brandy from the Cognac
region of south-western
France. Invented in the 17th
century, it is double-distilled
in pot stills and then aged
in new oak casks.

MINSTREL

INGREDIENTS

2 dashes of cognac

2 dashes of chilled vodka

1 dash of green crème de menthe

1 dash of Kahlua

Shake all of the ingredients very briefly with ice and strain into a shot glass.

DAME SHAMER

INGREDIENTS

1½ parts brandy

1 part cherry brandy

1 part Kahlua

1 part heavy cream

2 cocktail cherries, to garnish

Shake all ingredients with ice and strain into a highball glass over ice.

Garnish with two cocktail cherries on a swizzle stick.

PASSION

INGREDIENTS

½ part cherry brandy

½ part bourbon

½ part Passoã (passion fruit liqueur)

1½ parts cranberry juice

½ part coconut cream

2 cocktail cherries and coconut
   shavings, to garnish

Shake all of the ingredients with ice and double strain into a chilled

martini glass. Drop the cherries into the base of the glass and float the

coconut shavings on top of the drink.

FOX HOUND

INGREDIENTS

2 parts brandy

3 parts cranberry juice

½ part Kummel (see Trivia)

½ part freshly squeezed lime juice

Shake all ingredients with ice and strain over crushed ice into

a large goblet.

TRIVIA

*You may not have
heard of Kummel, but it
can be used to great effect
with brandy and also
bourbon. It is a clear liquid
distilled from grain and
flavored with caraway
and anise seeds.*

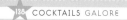

VINE

INGREDIENTS

2 parts cognac
1 part freshly pressed apple juice
½ part freshly squeezed grapefruit juice
1 dash of freshly squeezed lemon juice
1 dash of sugar syrup
4 seedless grapes
Grapefruit slices, to garnish

Muddle the grapes and sugar syrup in the base of a shaker. Add the remaining ingredients and shake with ice.

Strain the mix over ice into a highball glass, garnish with slices of grapefruit, and serve with straws.

PLAYMATE

INGREDIENTS

1 part brandy
1 part Grand Marnier
1 part apricot brandy
1 part freshly squeezed orange juice
½ egg white
4 drops of Angostura bitters
1 flaming orange spiral

Shake the liquid ingredients with ice and strain into a chilled martini

glass. Flambé an orange spiral over the drink and drop it in.

RED MARAUDER

INGREDIENTS

2 parts brandy

2 parts cranberry juice

$^1/_2$ part Chambord

(black raspberry liqueur)

1 dash of freshly squeezed lime juice

2 raspberries, to garnish

Shake all of the ingredients with ice and strain into a chilled martini glass.

Garnish with two raspberries on a swizzle stick.

APPLE CART MARTINI

INGREDIENTS

1$^1/_2$ parts apple brandy

1$^1/_2$ parts Cointreau

1 part freshly squeezed lemon juice

1 dash of sugar syrup

Apple wedge, to garnish

Shake all ingredients with ice and double strain into a chilled martini glass.

Garnish with an apple wedge on the rim.

TRIVIA

Apple brandy takes on different names depending on its origin. The French call it "calvados," most commonly produced in Normandy. However, in the USA, apple brandy is mostly known as "apple Jack."

BEST OF
THE REST

TOBLERONE

INGREDIENTS

1 part Bailey's Irish Cream
1 part Frangelico
½ part dark crème de cacao
½ part clear liquid honey
1 part heavy cream
1 teaspoon chocolate sauce

Blend the Bailey's, Frangelico, crème de cacao, honey, and cream with half a scoop of crushed ice. Take a hurricane glass and swirl chocolate sauce around the inner surface. Then pour in the creamy liquid and serve with straws.

TIJUANA CAFÉ

INGREDIENTS

5fl oz/160ml hot black coffee
1 part Kahlua or coffee liqueur
1 teaspoon sugar
3 parts heavy cream, lightly whipped
1 cinnamon stick

Pour the hot coffee into a warm heatproof coffee glass. Stir in the liqueur and sugar then spoon the lightly whipped cream on top so that it floats. Give it a gentle stir with a cinnamon stick and sprinkle with ground cinnamon.

SHERRY FLIP

INGREDIENTS
1 medium-sized egg
4 parts cream sherry

Shake or blend the egg and sherry with about 6 ice cubes until smooth.

Pour into a small goblet. Decorate the top with freshly grated nutmeg.

RAMBLER

INGREDIENTS
1 lime wedge
1 part gold rum
1 dash of Frangelico
1 dash of strawberry syrup
1 strawberry, to garnish

Squeeze the lime wedge into a cocktail shaker, then add the three liquid ingredients. Shake briefly with ice and double strain into a chilled shot glass. Drop the strawberry into the drink.

PIMM'S COCKTAIL

INGREDIENTS

1 part Pimm's No.1

3 parts lemonade

Cucumber slices

1 strawberry

Apple slices

Lemon slices

Orange slices

1 mint sprig, to garnish

Fill a highball glass with ice, then add the Pimm's. Put all of the garnishes

in the glass and top with the lemonade. Finish off with the mint sprig.

TIP

You know summer's arrived when your thoughts turn to refreshing Pimm's. Scale the ingredient measurements up using the same proportions, and build over ice in the largest pitcher you can find. The flavors of the garnishes, especially the mint and cucumber, really come out here as they have longer to marinate in the drink.

TRIVIA

It was way back in 1840 that Pimm's was first drunk and it still remains a favorite around the globe today. The classic Pimm's No. 1 is gin-based but early variations were made with whiskey, brandy, bourbon, and vodka. Make your Pimm's cocktail extra special by topping it with champagne instead of lemonade.

BAZOOKA JOE SHOOTER

INGREDIENTS

½ part blue curaçao
½ part crème de banane
  (banana liqueur)
½ part Irish cream liqueur

Pour the curaçao into a shot glass, followed by the crème de banane.
Float the Irish cream liqueur on top. The yellow crème de banane will sink
to the bottom and mix with the curaçao to create a luminous green layer
beneath the Irish cream.

TRIVIA

*Curaçao liqueurs are
traditionally made from the
dried peel of the small bitter
Curaçao orange, named after the
island of Curaçao in the Caribbean.
Curaçao liqueurs come in clear, red,
green, blue, and yellow. The colors
are purely decorative, but the
bitter orange flavors are
very similar.*

RED SKY AT NIGHT

INGREDIENTS

Dash of freshly squeezed lemon juice

7-up, to top

½ part crème de cassis
(black currant liqueur)

Fill a chilled highball glass with ice and add a good dash of lemon juice.

Pour in 7-up to almost fill the glass, and stir in the crème de cassis.

ENGLISH ROSE

INGREDIENTS

3 parts extra dry vermouth

1½ parts kirsch

1 part Parfait d'amour

1–2 rose petals, to garnish

Combine the ingredients in a mixing glass with cracked ice.

Stir well. Strain into a cocktail glass. Decorate by floating a rose petal

or two on top.

NATURAL BLONDE

INGREDIENTS

1 part Bailey's Irish Cream

1 part Grand Marnier

½ fresh mango or 1 part mango
  purée

1 fresh mango slice and 1 blackberry,
  to garnish

Blend the Bailey's, Grand Marnier, and mango together with a small scoop of crushed ice. Serve in a brandy

balloon glass garnished with a blackberry and a slice of fresh mango.

BATIDA GOIABA

INGREDIENTS

2 parts cachaca (Brazilian rum)

3 parts freshly squeezed (if possible)
  guava juice

1 dash of sugar syrup

1 dash of freshly squeezed lemon juice

Lemon slices, to garnish

Shake all of the liquid ingredients with ice and strain into a highball glass filled with crushed ice. Garnish with

slices of lemon and serve with straws.

TRIBBBLE

INGREDIENTS

½ part butterscotch schnapps

½ part crème de banane
  (banana liqueur)

½ part Bailey's Irish Cream

Layer the ingredients in the order

given above, with the Bailey's on top.

BELLINI

INGREDIENTS

3 parts chilled dry champagne

1 part chilled peach juice

1 peach slice, to garnish

Pour the champagne and peach juice into a chilled champagne saucer.

Stir lightly with a glass swizzle stick. Garnish with a thin slice of peach.

TRIVIA

*Invented in the
1940s at Harry's Bar in
Venice, the fragrant Bellini
cocktail really caught on with
Americans in the 1950s. Traditionally,
the Bellini is made with white peach
purée. For one of the best Bellinis
you'll ever taste, go to the world-
famous bar at the Savoy
Hotel, London.*

APPLEJACK

INGREDIENTS

1 part applejack

1 part grapefruit juice

Dash of grenadine

1 lemon spiral, to garnish

Stir or shake the ingredients with cracked ice. Strain into a cocktail glass

filled with crushed ice and serve with a spiral of lemon peel.

TRIVIA

The early American settlers distilled hard cider to make applejack and drank it neat. By the 1950s, however, tastes had become a little more refined.

ZESTY

INGREDIENTS

2 parts Frangelico
2 lime wedges

Fill a brandy balloon glass with crushed ice, add the Frangelico, then squeeze the two lime wedges into the drink, dropping them in as garnish. Serve with short straws.

SPARKLING BOUQUET

INGREDIENTS

1 part melon liqueur
Sparkling wine, to top
Flower petals, to garnish

Pour the melon liqueur into a cocktail glass or champagne saucer. Top with chilled sparkling wine and decorate with fragrant petals and flowers.

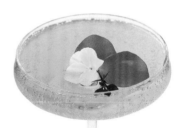

BUCK'S FIZZ

INGREDIENTS

2 parts orange juice

Champagne, to top

Pour the orange juice into a champagne flute and top with champagne.

TRIVIA

Also known as a
Mimosa, after the flowering
plant of the same color, this
refreshing cocktail has been around
since the 1920s. Some say it was
invented, as the Buck's Fizz, at the
Buck's Club in London. Others
claim it started as the Mimosa
at the Ritz Hotel Bar in
Paris.

PURPLE TURTLE

INGREDIENTS

½ part tequila

½ part blue curaçao

½ part sloe gin

Shake all of the ingredients briefly with ice and strain into a chilled shot glass.

GREEN FAIRY

INGREDIENTS

1 part absinthe

1 part freshly squeezed lemon juice

2 drops of Angostura bitters

½ egg white

½ part sugar syrup

1 part chilled water

Shake all of the ingredients with ice and strain into a chilled martini glass.

KIR

INGREDIENTS

½ part crème de cassis
  (black currant liqueur)
Chilled dry white wine, to top

Pour crème de cassis into a large chilled wine glass or goblet, then top with white wine and stir gently. Serve straight up.

TIP

The Kir was created by French farm laborers in Burgundy, who added crème de cassis to their Bourgogne Aligote wine to make it more palatable, and named the result after the colorful war hero and Mayor of Dijon, Canon Felix Kir. It's a quick and simple drink for a steamy summer's day. The usual ratio is 7 parts white wine to 1 part crème de cassis for a clean, crisp black currant flavor. If you're having a party, substitute champagne for white wine to create a Kir Royale.

ELECTRIC FLAG

INGREDIENTS

½ part grenadine syrup
½ part Parfait d'amour
½ part kirsch or grappa

Pour the grenadine syrup into the shot glass. Carefully add the Parfait d'amour, and then the kirsch or grappa, using a bar spoon if required.

MIDNIGHT RAMBLER

INGREDIENTS

2 parts Frangelico
2 parts Bailey's Irish Cream

Pour both ingredients over crushed ice in an old-fashioned glass, and serve with short straws.

A wonderful night-cap.

TEMPTING TRIO

INGREDIENTS
½ part green crème de menthe
(mint liqueur)
½ part crème de banane
(banana liqueur)
½ part Irish cream liqueur

Carefully layer the crème de menthe, crème de banane, and Irish cream liqueur into a shot glass using the reverse of a bar spoon.

CAIPIRINHA

INGREDIENTS
1 lime, segmented
1 teaspoon brown sugar
1 dash of sugar syrup
2 parts cachaca (Brazilian rum)

In a heavy-based old-fashioned glass, muddle the lime, brown sugar, and sugar syrup. Fill the glass with crushed ice, add cachaca, stir, and serve with straws and a stirrer.

TRIVIA
Caipirinha means "peasants' drink" in Brazil, where it is served in every bar. Cachaca is the Brazilian rum made from sugar cane—it is not as pure as most rums and retains the flavor of the raw ingredient.

RED HEAT

INGREDIENTS

½ part vodka
½ part peach schnapps
½ part Jägermeister
1 dash of cranberry juice

Shake all of the ingredients briefly with ice and strain into a shot glass.

LOCH ALMOND

INGREDIENTS

1½ parts amaretto
1½ parts Scotch whisky
Ginger ale, to top
1 amaretti biscuit, to garnish

Build the ingredients over ice in a highball glass. Stir and float the biscuit

as the garnish.

MEXICAN MARSHMALLOW MOCHA

INGREDIENTS

2 teaspoons cocoa powder,
   plus a little extra as a garnish
1 part Kahlua
Hot filter coffee, to top
2 marshmallows and whipped
   cream, to garnish

Put the cocoa powder in the base of a toddy glass, add the Kahlua and coffee, then stir to dissolve. Drop two

marshmallows in, and float the cream over these. Dust the surface with cocoa powder.

GREEK LIGHTNING

INGREDIENTS

½ part ouzo
½ part vodka
½ part Chambord
   (black raspberry liqueur)

Shake all of the ingredients together and strain into a shot glass. Best served for more than one person.

FLATLINER

INGREDIENTS

¹/₂ part sambuca

4 drops of Tabasco sauce

¹/₂ part gold tequila

In a shot glass, layer the ingredients in the order above, finishing with the

tequila. Down in one.

PASSIONATE PEACH FIZZ

INGREDIENTS

2 parts orange juice

2 parts passion fruit juice

¹/₂ part peach schnapps

Champagne or sparkling wine, to top

Peach slice, to garnish

Shake the fruit juices and the peach schnapps vigorously in a

cocktail shaker with cracked ice. Strain into a champagne flute and

top with champagne or sparkling wine. Serve straight up with

a thin slice of peach.

GREEN HORNET

INGREDIENTS

½ part Pisang Ambon
  (banana-based liqueur)
½ part vodka
1 tiny dash of absinthe
1 dash of lime cordial

Shake all of the ingredients very briefly with ice and double strain into

a chilled shot glass.

INDULGENCE

INGREDIENTS

½ part amaretto
½ part dark crème de cacao
½ part Amarula Cream Liqueur

In a shot glass, layer the ingredients in the order above,

finishing with the Amarula.

TRIVIA

Amaretto is an almond-based liqueur dating back to 16th-century Italy, and thought to have been created by a student of Leonardo da Vinci. The most popular brand, Disaronno, has a sweet taste of vanilla and marzipan.

NONALCOHOLIC

COOL DUDE

INGREDIENTS
1 part freshly squeezed lime juice
7-up, to top
Slices of lime and lemon frozen in
    ice cubes

Pour the lime juice into an old-fashioned glass half-filled with

the decorated ice cubes. Top with 7-up and stir well.

NUTTY PLUM SMOOTHIE

INGREDIENTS
2 plums
¼ cup/35g raspberries
1 tablespoon ground almonds
1 tablespoon sesame seeds
¼ cup/60ml water
Raspberries, to garnish

Cut around the crease of the plums, then twist apart and lever out the

pit. Roughly chop the flesh. Place the chopped plums in a blender with

the raspberries, ground almonds, sesame seeds, and water, and blend

for about 1 minute until smooth and creamy. Pour the smoothie into

a glass and serve.

CRANBERRY GROVE

INGREDIENTS

2 parts cranberry juice
Dash of freshly squeezed lemon juice
Orange soda or ginger ale, to top
Slices of orange and lemon, to garnish

Pour the juice into a highball glass, half-filled with ice cubes, then top

with orange soda or ginger ale. Garnish with slices of orange and lemon.

BLACKBERRY SPICE

INGREDIENTS

1 cinnamon stick
$1/2$ cup/120ml boiling water
$1^1/_2$ well-flavored dessert apples
$1/2$ cup/75g blackberries

Put the cinnamon and boiling water in a small pan, bring to a boil, and then simmer gently for about 5 minutes.

Leave to cool for 10 minutes. Remove and reserve the cinnamon stick. Roughly chop the apples. Press the

blackberries through a juicer, followed by the apples, and then stir the cooled cinnamon water into the juice.

Pour into a glass and serve with the cinnamon stick.

TROPICAL GLOW

INGREDIENTS

½ large papaya
¼ large pineapple (about 9oz/250g),
   plus extra to garnish
1 large carrot, trimmed

Scoop out the seeds from the papaya, then cut the flesh into wedges and remove the skin. Cut off the skin from the pineapple and discard, then cut the flesh away from the central core and discard the core. Cut the carrot into rough chunks. Press the papaya through a juicer, followed by the pineapple and carrot. Stir the juice, pour into a tall glass, add a wedge of pineapple and serve.

BERRY BRIGHT EYES

INGREDIENTS

3 strawberries
1 pear
¼ cup/35g raspberries
¼ cup/40g blueberries
Ice, to serve
Berries, to garnish

Halve any large strawberries and roughly chop the pear into large chunks. Press the berries through the juicer, followed by the chunks of pear, and then pour into a glass filled with ice. Garnish with berries and serve.

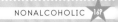

PEACH & CHERRY PLEASURE

INGREDIENTS

2 peaches

$^1\!/_3$ cup/60g cherries

$^1\!/_2$ cup/90g red grapes

Put the peaches in a bowl, pour over boiling water to cover and leave for 30 seconds. Drain and peel. Cut around the crease of each peach, twist the two sides apart and lever out the pit. Chop the flesh. Remove the cherry pits using a cherry-pitter, then put the cherries and peaches in a blender. Push the grapes through a juicer, and then pour the juice into the blender and blend for 30 seconds until smooth. Pour into a glass and serve.

KIWI & BANANA SMOOTHIE

INGREDIENTS

1 kiwi fruit

$^1\!/_2$ banana

$^1\!/_2$ part vanilla syrup

4 parts milk

Kiwi slices, to garnish

Blend all of the liquid ingredients with a small scoop of ice and pour into a highball glass. Garnish with kiwi slices and serve with straws.

CHOCOLATE-GINGER SWIRL

INGREDIENTS
6 dates, chopped
½ cup/120ml boiling water
1 piece stem ginger in syrup, chopped
1oz/25g bittersweet chocolate
7oz/200g silken tofu
1 tablespoon soya milk
Chocolate shavings, to decorate

Place the dates in a bowl, pour over the boiling water and leave to soak for 30 minutes. Place the dates and soaking liquid in a blender, add the ginger and process for about 1 minute until the mixture is smooth. Put the chocolate in a bowl over a pan of simmering water and heat until melted. Remove the bowl from the pan and very slowly pour in the date mixture, stirring continuously until thoroughly mixed. Chill for about 10 minutes. Meanwhile, rinse out the blender, then add half the tofu and the soya milk. Blend for about 1 minute, or until smooth and frothy. Tip the mixture into a pitcher and rinse out the blender. Pour the chocolate mixture into the blender, add the remaining tofu and blend until combined. Spoon alternate layers of the chocolate and soya mixtures into an old-fashioned glass and decorate with chocolate shavings.

RED-HOT STRAWBERRY JUICE

INGREDIENTS

2 blood oranges
1 red bird's eye chili, seeded
    and finely chopped, plus 1 chili
    to garnish
Scant ½ cup/60g strawberries, hulled

Squeeze the juice from the oranges and pour into a blender. Add the
chopped chili and strawberries, and blend for about 45 seconds. Pour into
a small glass, garnish with an extra chili, and sip slowly.

APPLE WISE

INGREDIENTS

4fl oz/125ml sparkling apple juice
Ginger ale, to top
1 apple wedge, to garnish

Half fill a highball glass with ice cubes. Pour in the apple juice to
three quarters fill the glass. Top with ginger ale. Garnish with a
wedge of apple.

AMBER FIZZ

INGREDIENTS
4fl oz US/125ml orange juice
Ginger ale, to top
Orange rind, to garnish

Fill an old-fashioned glass with ice then half fill with orange juice. Top
with ginger ale. Float a piece of pared orange rind on top to garnish.

TROPICAL TEASER

INGREDIENTS
1 lemongrass stalk
¼ cup/60ml water
1 cup/50g lychees
½ mango
½ papaya
½ cup/90g white grapes

Gently crush the lemongrass stalk, then place in a small pan with the water. Bring to the boil, then simmer for
2 minutes. Leave to cool. Meanwhile, peel the lychees and remove the black pits. Peel the mango and chop the
flesh. Scoop out the seeds from the papaya, then peel and chop the flesh. Press the fruit through a juicer. Strain
the lemongrass water into the juice and stir.

MELON MIRAGE

INGREDIENTS

A wedge of watermelon
(about ⅛ melon)
1 slice fresh pineapple
1 part sugar syrup
Dash of freshly squeezed lime juice

Cut two small wedges from the wedge of watermelon
and a wedge out of the pineapple slice, and set aside
for garnish. Peel the watermelon, remove the seeds,
and peel the pineapple and remove the core. Put the
fruit in a blender with crushed ice. Blend until almost
smooth, adding sugar syrup and a dash of lime juice to
make a pink, frothy mixture. Pour into a chilled
highball glass. Garnish with watermelon and pineapple
wedges and a pineapple leaf.

ICY INDULGENCE

INGREDIENTS

1 cup/150g frozen soft fruits, such
   as blackberries, blueberries,
   cherries and black currants,
   plus extra to garnish
1 cup almond milk

Leave the frozen fruit at room temperature for about 5 minutes to thaw
slightly, then tip into a blender with the almond milk. Blend until smooth
and slushy, and then pour into a glass. Garnish with a spoonful of frozen
fruits and serve immediately.

APRICOT SWEETIE

INGREDIENTS

¼ cup/50g ready-to-eat dried apricots
1 tablespoon sunflower seeds
⅔ cup/160ml live plain yogurt
⅓ cup/80ml milk
1 teaspoon clear honey
2 teaspoons lemon juice
Orange slice, to garnish

Roughly chop the apricots and put in a blender with the sunflower seeds,
yogurt, milk, honey, and lemon juice. Blend the ingredients together for
1–2 minutes until really smooth and creamy. Pour into a glass, then sit
back and enjoy. Garnish with a slice of orange on the rim of the glass.

VIRGINITY

INGREDIENTS

4 parts cranberry juice
1 dash of black currant cordial
$\frac{1}{2}$ part freshly squeezed lemon juice
3 parts freshly pressed apple juice
Watermelon wedges, to garnish

Blend all of the ingredients with a small scoop of crushed ice and serve in a highball glass with straws. Garnish with wedges of fresh watermelon.

DREAMY BLUEBERRY RIPPLE

INGREDIENTS

$\frac{2}{3}$ cup/160ml live plain yogurt
3 tablespoons milk
1 teaspoon clear honey, plus extra for
    drizzling
$\frac{1}{2}$ cup/90g red grapes
$\frac{1}{2}$ cup/80g blueberries
$1\frac{1}{2}$ teaspoons lime juice

Beat together the yogurt, milk, and honey, then set aside. Push the grapes through a juicer and pour the juicer into a blender. Reserve two or three blueberries, then add the rest to the blender. Blend to make a smooth purée. Add lime juice to taste. Spoon alternating layers of the yogurt and blueberry mixtures into a tall glass to give a rippled effect, finishing with a spoonful of the yogurt mixture. Drizzle over a little more honey and decorate with the reserved blueberries.

CHINESE CHEER

INGREDIENTS
1 part freshly squeezed lime juice
1 part freshly squeezed lemon juice
1 teaspoon finely grated fresh
   ginger root
1½ parts sugar syrup
1 star anise ice cube
Sparkling water, to top

Combine the lime and lemon juices with the ginger and sugar syrup in
a cocktail shaker. Shake vigorously with cracked ice. Strain into a chilled
old-fashioned glass. Add decorated ice cube and top with sparkling water.

ICED TEA DANCE

INGREDIENTS
3fl oz/100ml cooled fruit tea
   (made with one teabag)
Sprite or 7-up, to top
Segments of tangerine frozen in
   ice cubes

Pour the cold "tea" into a chilled toddy glass, and add four
decorated ice cubes. Top with Sprite or 7-up.

PASSIONATE PROTECTOR

INGREDIENTS

2 passion fruit, plus extra to garnish
2 carrots, trimmed
1 orange

Halve the passion fruits and scoop the pulp into a strainer placed over a pitcher. Using the back of a spoon, press the pulp into the pitcher. Cut the carrot into rough chunks. Peel the orange and divide into quarters, then press the orange and carrots through a juicer. Stir the juice into the passion fruit pulp. Pour into a tall glass and drink immediately.

TOMATO PEP

INGREDIENTS

½ apple
1 sprig fresh thyme, plus extra
   to garnish
1½ tablespoons chopped fresh basil
1 teaspoon chopped fresh mint
1½ cups/250g baby tomatoes

Roughly chop the apple and strip the leaves off the thyme sprig. Press the herbs through a juicer followed by the apple, then press through the tomatoes. (Be careful as the baby tomatoes have a tendency to shoot back out of some juicers!) Stir the juice, pour into a glass, garnish with thyme leaves, and serve immediately.

GRAPEVINE

INGREDIENTS

Small bunch of frozen grapes
3 parts grape juice
Bitter lemon soda, to top

Put the frozen grapes into a chilled goblet. Pour in the grape juice, top

with bitter lemon soda, and serve straight up.

STRAWBERRY BALSAMICO

INGREDIENTS

5 fresh ripe strawberries
½ part sugar syrup
Dash of balsamic vinegar
Freshly ground black pepper

Combine the strawberries with the sugar syrup and four ice cubes in a

blender. Blend until puréed. Pour into a highball glass filled with ice cubes.

Add a dash of balsamic vinegar and a grind of black pepper. Garnish with

a basil leaf and a strawberry. Freeze basil leaves in the ice cubes for extra

flavor and effect.

FIGGY PLUM SMOOTHIE

INGREDIENTS

1 rosemary sprig
$^1/_2$ cup/120ml water
3 figs
2 plums
1 teaspoon lemon juice
$^3/_4$ cup/180ml strained plain yogurt
Clear honey, to drizzle

Strip the leaves from the rosemary sprig and place them in a mortar. Lightly bruise the leaves with a pestle, then tip the leaves into a small pan. Add the water, bring to the boil, and then simmer very gently for 3 minutes. Remove the pan from the heat and leave to steep for about 5 minutes. Strain the liquid into a bowl and leave to cool. Meanwhile, halve the figs and scoop the flesh into a blender. Cut around the crease of the plums and twist to pull apart. Lever out the pit using the tip of the knife, then roughly chop the flesh and add to the blender. Add the cooled rosemary water and blend until smooth. Stir in the lemon juice to taste. Spoon a dollop of yogurt into a tall glass, and then pour over a little of the smoothie, add another dollop of yogurt, and then pour over more smoothie. Continue in this way to create a marbled effect. Finish with a dollop of yogurt, and then drizzle over a little honey and serve.

GREEN SPIDER

INGREDIENTS
10fl oz/300ml lemonade
Pistachio ice cream
Dash of mint cordial

Fill a highball with crushed ice then add the lemonade. Float a scoop of

pistachio ice cream on top and drizzle mint cordial. Serve with a straw.

MELON MAGIC

INGREDIENTS
⅓ Ogen melon
3 apricots
1 tablespoon pumpkin seeds
¼ teaspoon ginkgo biloba extract
2–3 tablespoons water

Scoop out the melon seeds and discard, then scoop the flesh into a blender. Cut around the crease in the

apricots, and then twist the two halves apart and lever out the pits. Roughly chop the flesh and place in the

blender. Add the pumpkin seeds and ginkgo biloba extract and blend for about 1 minute to make a smooth

purée. Stir in a little water and serve in a tall glass.

COCONUT ICE

INGREDIENTS

1 piece stem ginger in syrup,
   plus 2 teaspoons syrup from the jar
¾ cup/180ml coconut milk
½ lime
Lime wedge, to garnish
Crushed ice, to serve

Finely chop the stem ginger, then place in a blender with the coconut milk and ginger syrup. Squeeze in the juice from the lime. Blend very briefly to combine. (Just give it one blitz because overblending will cause the mixture to separate.) Fill a tall glass with crushed ice and pour over the smoothie. Garnish with the lime wedge and serve.

VAMPIRE JUICE

INGREDIENTS

½ orange
1 tomato
1 large beet
1 garlic clove, peeled
1 celery stick

Remove the peel from the orange and chop the tomato and beet into rough chunks. Press the garlic through a juicer, followed by the orange, beet, tomato, and celery. Stir the juice, pour into a small glass and sip slowly.

PINK PASSION

INGREDIENTS

3 oranges
1/2 cup/80g raspberries
1 passion fruit
Crushed ice, to serve

Remove the peel from the oranges and cut into rough chunks. Press the raspberries through a juicer followed by the oranges. Cut the passion fruit in half and scoop the pulp into the juice. Stir to combine, and then pour the juice into a tall glass filled with crushed ice.

LAVENDER & WATERMELON WIND-DOWN

INGREDIENTS

1/2 teaspoon lavender flowers
1/4 cup/60ml boiling water
12oz/350g watermelon
1/2 cup/90g red grapes
Lavender stalks, to garnish

Put the lavender in a small bowl and pour over the boiling water. Leave to stand for about 10 minutes, then strain the flavored water into a pitcher and discard the flowers. Cut the rind from the watermelon and cut the flesh into large chunks. Press the watermelon through a juicer, followed by the red grapes, then stir in the lavender water. Pour the juice into a glass, garnish with the lavender stalks and serve immediately.

MINT HAZE

INGREDIENTS
2 teaspoons sugar
5 mint leaves
Dash of freshly squeezed lime juice
Sparkling apple juice, to top

Crush the sugar and mint leaves in a pestle and mortar. Frost the rim of an old-fashioned glass by dipping it in water then in the mint sugar. Put a little more mint sugar in the glass, with three or four ice cubes. Add a dash of lime juice, then top with sparkling apple juice. Freeze mint leaves in the ice cubes for extra flavor and effect.

GAZPACHO

INGREDIENTS
6fl oz/180ml tomato juice
1 inch/2.5cm piece of cucumber, peeled, seeds removed
1 inch/2.5cm piece of celery
1 small roasted red pepper
Small pinch of dried chili flakes
Dash of freshly squeezed lemon juice

Combine ingredients in a blender with 4 or 5 ice cubes. Blend until smooth, and pour into a highball or Collins glass, half-filled with ice. Garnish with a celery stick, cucumber slices, basil leaves, and a cherry tomato. Freeze basil leaves in the ice cubes for extra flavor and effect.

BAMBOOZLE

INGREDIENTS

3 parts guava juice
2 parts orange juice
2 parts passion fruit juice
Dash of freshly squeezed lime juice
Club soda (optional)
Bamboo sprig, to garnish

Combine juices with cracked ice in a cocktail shaker. Shake vigorously.

Strain into a bamboo-style highball glass, half-filled with crushed ice.

Top with a little club soda if desired. Garnish with a sprig of bamboo.

BARBIE GIRL

INGREDIENTS

A little pink coloring and sugar, for frosting
5 very large ripe strawberries
1 slice pineapple
1 part orange juice
1 part freshly squeezed lemon juice
Strawberry slices, to garnish

Frost the top of a large chilled cocktail glass by dipping it in coloring then in sugar. Combine the fruit and juices in a blender, with four or five ice cubes. Blend until smooth. Pour into the frosted glass and garnish with slices of strawberry.

INDEX

A

Ab Fab 24

Acapulco Gold 72

Alexander 67

Alexander's Sister 60

Almond Breeze 73

Amber Fizz 173

Apple Cart Martini 139

Applejack 151

Apple Wise 172

Apricot Sweetie 175

Arizona Cooler 66

Arthur Tompkins 51

Austin Powers 72

Avalon 28

Aviation 57

B

B&B 135

Bacardi 78

Baja Sour 95

Bamboozle 187

Banana Daiquiri 79

Barbie Girl 187

Basil Vice 39

Batida Goiaba 148

Bazooka Joe Shooter 146

Bellini 150

Berry Bright Eyes 168

Between the Sheets 121

Big City Dog 134

Blackberry Spice 167

Black Widow 84

Bloody Mary 25

Blue Angel 120

Blue Blazer 117

Border Crossing 97

Brandy Crusta 132

Brandy Fix 124

Breakfast Martini 64

Bronx 55

Buck's Fizz 153

Buck's Twizz 32

Bumble Bee 50

C

Caipirinha 158

Canchanchara 70

Cape Codder 24

Caribbean Champagne
  Cocktail 122

Chi-Chi 35

Chin Chin 106

Chinese Cheer 178

Chocolate-Ginger Swirl 170

Cielo 35

Classic Cocktail 123

Classic Irish Coffee 116

Clover Club 48

Coconut Ice 184

Colonel T 108

Cool Dude 166

Coq Rouge 51

Cosmopolitan 44

Cranberry Grove 167

CranKiss 45

Cuba Libre 83

Cuban Peach 70

D

Dame Shamer 131

Dangerous Detox 26

Desperado 98

Double Vision 43

Dreamy Blueberry Ripple 177

Dry Martini 57

Dubonnet Cocktail 54

E

Easy Tiger 100

Electric Flag 157

English Rose 147

F

Festive Flare 71

'57 Chevy 27

Figgy Plum Smoothie 181

Fireball 116

Flatliner 162

Forest Fruit 96

Fox Hound 136

French 90 128

Frisco 105

Frisky Buck 115

Frontier 113

Frozen Strawberry Margarita 90

G

Gazpacho 186

Gibson Martini 55

Gimlet 59

Gin Geenie 63

Gin Sour 64

Glitterati 42

Godfather Sour 110

Grapevine 180

Greek Lightning 160

Greenback 52

Green Fairy 155

Green Hornet 163

Green Spider 182

Grenada 87

H

Harvey Wallbanger 27

Havana Beach 83

Havana Cocktail 76

Hedgerow Sling 66

Honeysuckle 74

I

Iced Tea Dance 178

Icy Indulgence 175

Ignorance 33

Incognito 122

Indulgence 163

Invitation Only 63

J

Jaffa 124

K

Kalashnikov 99

Kentucky Cream Tea 117

Kir 156

Kitsch Revolt 37

Kiwi & Banana Smoothie 169

Kiwi Kraze 49

Knickerbocker 77

L

Lavender & Watermelon
  Wind-Down 185

Lemon Meringue Martini 30

Limoncello Italiano 45

Loch Almond 159

Long Island Iced Tea 31

Loretto Lemonade 112

M

Madras 43

Maiden's Blush 67

Mai Tai 76

Manhattan 106

Margarita 90

Melon Magic 182

Melon Mirage 174

Mexican Marshmallow
  Mocha 160

Maxim 60

Mexican Wave 92

Miami 82

Midnight Rambler 157

Millionaire 105

Minstrel 131

Mint Haze 186

Mint Julep 113

Mojito 74

Morello Bourbon Daiquiri 115

Moscow Mule 38

Moulin Rouge 129

Mudslide 32

N

Natural Blonde 148

Nice Pear 120

Not Tonight Josephine 128

Nutty Plum Smoothie 166

O

Off-Shore 98

Old-Fashioned 107

Opal Martini 56

Orange Blossom 56

P

Paradise Martini 48

Park Avenue 49

Passion 136

Passionate Peach Fizz 162

Passionate Protector 179

Passion Fruit Margarita 91

Peach & Cherry Pleasure 169

Peach Brandy Smash 135

Petite Martini 126

Pimm's Cocktail 145

Piña Colada 82

Pink Passion 185

Pisco Sour 123

Plasma 40

Planters' Punch 87

Playmate 138

Polish Martini 44

Pot Shot 40

Presidente 79

Purple Turtle 155

R

Rambler 143

Rapaska 30

Raspberry Collins 59

Raspberry Crush 54

Raspberry Lynchburg 108

Red Heat 159

Red-Hot Strawberry Juice 172

Red Marauder 139

Red October 33

Red Sky at Night 147

Renaissance 134

Rhett Butler 111

Rising Sun 28

Russian Spring Punch 42

Rusty Nail 104

S

Saketini 37

Sazerac 110

Sea Mist 36

Sherry Flip 143

Sidecar 126

Silky Pin 107

Singapore Sling 62

Sloe Gin & Tonic 50

Solera Eclipse 111

Sol Y Sombre 132

Sour Apple 97

Sparkling Bouquet 152

Stinger 127

Strawberry Balsamico 180

Strawberry Daiquiri 81

T

Tempting Trio 158

Tequila Slammer 99

Tequila Sunrise 93

Tequini 96

Thigh High 95

Tijuana Café 142

Tijuana Sling 92

Toblerone 142

Tomato Pep 179

Tom Collins 61

Traditional Sangria 127

Tre 77

Tribbble 150

Tropical Glow 168

Tropical Teaser 173

V

Vampire Juice 184

Vesper 38

Victory Collins 26

Vine 138

Virginity 177

W

West Indian Iced Tea 78

Whisky Mac 104

Whiskey Sour 112

White Russian 36

White Wine Cooler 133

White Witch 84

Windward Island 86

Z

Zesty 152

Zombie 86

RECIPE CREDITS

Allan Gage

Pages 24 lower; 26 lower; 27 upper; 28; 30 upper; 32 lower; 33 upper; 35; 37 lower; 38 lower; 40; 42 upper; 43 lower; 44 upper; 45 upper; 48 lower; 49 upper; 50 upper; 51 lower; 52; 55 upper; 56 lower; 57 upper; 59–60; 63–4; 66; 67 lower; 70 lower; 74; 77 lower; 78 lower; 79 lower; 81; 83 upper; 84; 87 upper; 90 lower; 91; 92 upper; 95–100; 104 lower; 106 upper; 107 lower; 108; 110 lower; 111; 112 lower; 113 upper; 115; 116 upper; 117 lower; 120 upper; 122 upper; 123 upper; 124; 126 upper; 127 lower; 128 upper; 131; 132 lower; 134–6; 138–9; 142 upper; 143 lower; 148; 150 upper; 152 upper; 155; 157 lower; 158 lower; 159–60; 162 upper; 163; 160 lower; 169 lower; 177 upper.

Kate Moseley

Pages 24 upper; 25; 26 upper; 27 lower; 30 lower; 31; 32 upper; 33 lower; 36; 37 upper; 38 upper; 39; 42 lower; 43 upper; 44 lower; 45 lower; 48 upper; 49 lower; 50 lower; 51 upper; 54; 55 lower; 56 upper; 57 upper; 61–2; 67 upper; 70 upper; 71–3; 76; 77 upper; 78 upper; 79 upper; 82; 83 lower; 86; 87 lower; 90 upper; 92 lower; 93; 104 upper; 105; 106 lower; 107 upper; 110 upper; 112 upper; 113 lower; 116 lower; 117 upper; 120 lower; 121; 122 lower; 123 lower; 126 lower; 127 upper; 128 lower; 129; 132 upper; 133; 142 lower; 143 upper; 146–7; 150 lower; 151; 152 lower; 153; 156; 157 upper; 158 upper; 162 lower; 166 upper; 167 upper; 172 lower; 173 upper; 174; 178; 180; 186; 187.

Susannah Blake

Pages 166 lower; 167 lower; 168; 169 upper; 170; 172 upper; 173 lower; 175; 177 lower; 179; 181; 182 lower; 184–185.

PHOTOGRAPHY CREDITS

Simon Pask

Pages 29; 34; 41; 53; 58; 60; 65–6; 75; 80; 85; 91; 94; 97–9; 101; 109; 111; 114; 125; 130; 135; 137; 138; 143 lower; 144; 149; 152 upper; 154; 159; 161; 171; 176; 183.

Chris Alack

Pages 24–7; 30–3; 36; 38–9; 42–5; 48–51; 54–7; 61–2; 67; 70–3; 76–79; 82–3; 86–7; 90; 92–3; 104–7; 110; 112–3; 116–7; 120–3; 126–9; 132–3; 142; 143 upper; 146–7; 150–1; 152 lower; 153; 156–8; 162; 166 upper; 167; 172 lower; 173–4; 178; 180; 186–7.

Janine Hosegood

Pages 166 lower; 168–9; 172 upper; 175; 179; 181; 184–5.